ANTICRAFT

RENÉE RIGDON

ZABET STEWART

Knitting,
Beading and
Stitching for the
Slightly Sinister

NORTH LIGHT BOOKS

CINCINNATI, OHIO

Anticraft Copyright © 2007 by Renée Rigdon
and Zabet Stewart. Manufactured in China. All
rights reserved. No part of this book may be
reproduced in any form or by any electronic or
mechanical means including information stor-
age and retrieval systems without permission in
writing from the publisher, except by a review-
er, who may quote a brief passage in review.
Published by North Light Books, an imprint
of F+W Publications, Inc., 4700 East Galbraith
Road, Cincinnati, Ohio 45236. (800) 289-0963.
First edition.

11 10 09 08 07   5 4 3 2 1

Distributed in Canada by Fraser Direct
100 Armstrong Avenue
Georgetown, ON, Canada L7G 5S4
Tel: (905) 877-4411

Distributed in the U.K. and Europe by David &
Charles
Brunel House, Newton Abbot, Devon, TQ12
4PU, England
Tel: (+44) 1626 323200, Fax: (+44) 1626 323319
Email: postmaster@davidandcharles.co.uk

Distributed in Australia by Capricorn Link
P.O. Box 704, S. Windsor, NSW 2756 Australia
Tel: (02) 4577-3555

Library of Congress Cataloging-in-Publication
Data

Rigdon, Renée.
  Anticraft : knitting, beading, and stitching for
the slightly sinister / Renée Rigdon and Zabet
Stewart.
      p. cm.
  Includes index.
  ISBN-13: 978-1-60061-030-1 (pbk. : alk. paper)
  ISBN-10: 1-60061-030-7 (pbk. : alk. paper)
  1. Knitting. 2. Beadwork. I. Stewart, Zabet. II.
Title.
  TT820.R563 2007
  746.43'2--dc22

                              2007027648

EDITOR:
Tonia Davenport

DESIGNER:
Maya Drozdz

PHOTOGRAPHER:
Al Parrish

**PRODUCTION
COORDINATOR:**
Greg Nock

STYLISTS:
Leslie Brinkley
Maya Drozdz

HAIR AND MAKEUP:
Cass Smith

COMIC ILLUSTRATOR:
Matt Rigdon
www.fluffyandbear.com

www.fwbookstore.com

Some digital brushes in this book are courtesy of Jason Gaylor of designfruit.com.

Dedication

For Cayden, who will now know beyond a shadow
of a doubt that his mother was never cool.
—Renée

For Grandma Amy, who didn't teach me how
to knit. Which, strangely enough, is how I got
started down this path.
—Zabet

CONTENTS

Antifesto

We were deep in the clutches of a weeklong absinthe binge[1] when the Divine Hand of Brilliance touched us in an inappropriate place. When this vision came, we knew we must create a haven for all the sinister crafters of the world. No more would we be cowed into silence by cheerful scrapbook stickers. Never again would we be forced to gleefully execute a sweater of intarsia puppies. The Green Fairy had blessed us with an exotic vision we were powerless to deny. We madly scrambled for pen and paper with which to compose our opus. Finding none, we took up our knitting needles and carved text into the walls.[2] With an old tube of Vamp[3] we illustrated our glorious creation.[4] Upon release from the hospital, we returned to our lives with renewed direction and embarked upon this project with the fervor of a snake-kissing Pentecostal who has an anti-venom kit.[5]

But not really. Really, we were thrilled when crafting was de-grannified[6]; we just got tired of it having to be so dang perky all the time. We suppose that's what happens when you take something old into the marketing department for cosmetic surgery. Some things get sucked out, some things get porcelain veneers, and some things get, um, perkier.[7]

Creation from chaos is natural. We've come to a place where we've realized that we have this actual, physical need to create things. We've discovered that we hate people *en masse*,[8] we're sick of homogenized culture, and these realizations have left holes in our hearts.[9] We create to fill those holes, to be able to sleep at night knowing we've done something, even a small something, to confront the manufactured culture that is currently being churned out.[10]

The point then is not that you should craft just like us.[11] You should craft in the medium that understands you.[12] This is just a place to let your eyes rest, find some inspiration, or scream yourself hoarse. We're all outcasts and refugees from the mainstream here. We're strange girls, tactless and profane in the face of the sacred, obsessed with mortality and the things you find under flesh and over bone. Our personalities are in this (can you tell that one of us likes puns?[13]), which makes it personal. We want you to help us carry this along, which makes it political—a stand against the current trends in society to sanitize grief, drug sadness, hide obscenities, stigmatize sex, and take everything much, *much* too seriously.[14]

6

This is a lie. We did make some absinthe once, but it was too horrible to actually drink.

[2] Also a lie.

[3] A seriously old tube. Like 1990 old. Gross.

[4] Again, a lie. Why are you considering taking craft advice from such pathological liars?

[5] We live in Kentucky—we know of what we speak here—but, also a lie.

[6] Yes, we know *your* grandmother is cool. Ours are as well.

[7] If you don't know what we're talking about, put this book down and walk away.

Zabet *really* hates people.

[9] We'll wax poetic if we want to.

[10] Skatchamogowza!

[11] Yes, you should. We know what's best for you.

[12] We're still waiting for wood-enamel, gold-leaf bookbinding in a Jell-O mold project.

[13] Not yet, but you will.

[14] Seriously? You read all these footnotes? And we thought we were, uh, different.

7

was spent stroking each other's egos; and the final five percent was spent writing it. We hope you enjoy our five percent effort.

—Renée and Zabet

9

TING

Knitting was invented in 2001 by Debbie Stoller.[1] She dreamt of an empire of robot slaves, making what she was told in a vision would be called "scarves." The first scarf was manufactured in 2002[2], but unfortunately robot slaves hadn't been invented yet, so she had to do it herself. It was a wondrous scarf, and it shone light and warmth down on the world. Wait, no, that's the sun. The scarf was really nice though. With fringe, even. Since the creation of knitting, it has become a favorite pastime of yoga teachers looking for more media coverage. Some—losers—even say it is the new yoga. The old yoga was, of course, yoga. And binge drinking. Binge drinking is liver yoga, but has nothing to do with knitting. Unless you are Lucy Neatby, creator of "Cables After Whiskey."

[1] Lie.
[2] Not exactly accurate either.

11

SNAKE DANCE THIGH HIGHS

BY SEVERINA

Thigh-high stockings in a luscious silk/wool blend yarn with lace snakes meandering down the back seam—the next best thing to having real, live snakes sneaking out of your skirts. These can be clipped up using metal old-style garters (don't bother with the cheap plastic ones), or you can rig up something fun with kids' mitten clips.

MOOD ENHANCERS:

"Marco Polo," *Live in Paris and Toronto* by Loreena McKennitt

SKILLS USED:

Basic knitting (see page 131)
Mathematical acrobatics

MATERIALS AND TOOLS:

8 oz (2,520 yards or 2,268 meters) JaggerSpun Zephyr 2/18 wool/silk blend in Ebony
1 set US #2 (2.75mm) double-point needles (or size needed to obtain gauge)
Stitch marker
Tapestry needle

GAUGE:

36 st × 40 rows = 4" (10cm) in stockinette stitch with two strands of yarn held together

FINISHED SIZE:

Size: M/L
Completed stocking length: 27" (69cm)
Circumference of thigh: 18"–20" (46cm–51cm)
Snake length: 17" (43cm)
See *Resizing* at the end of the pattern if you are brave enough to muck about with it.

NOTES:

Two strands were held together throughout. Any two-ply Shetland lace-weight or cobweb yarn can be substituted but please make sure you check your gauge. One-hundred percent silk or cotton yarns can be used but they will have much less stretch than one-hundred percent wool or wool blends. Try an elastic sock yarn for extra slinkiness. If you are completely insane and have a year with nothing better to do you can use one strand and size 000 needles. This would probably turn the snake into an earthworm. Perfect if you've got a jones for earthworms. I made a valiant stab at that version but realized that perhaps I did need to stop knitting and maybe sleep occasionally.

RIGHT STOCKING

Cuff:

With two strands of yarn held together, cast on 108 sts loosely. Divide evenly between three needles (36 sts per needle). Join together in a round without twisting the sts. Work in 2×2 ribbing (K2, P2) for 1" (3cm), or desired length.

Next Round: K all sts.

Work all rounds of the edging chart (see page 16).

Leg:

Set Up Round: K15, Ssk, K1, Pm, P1, K1, K2tog, K remaining sts.

Round 1, 3, and 5: K all sts.

Round 2 and 4: K to marker, slip marker, P1, K remaining sts.

Round 6: K to 3 sts before marker, Ssk, K1, slip marker, P1, K1, K2tog, K remaining sts.

Repeat Rounds 1–6 a total of five times, or to desired length. 96 sts remain.

Work all rounds of Right Stocking Chart. 62 sts remain.

Work in stockinette stitch with purl-stitch seam (purling in the st after the marker every other round) until stocking is 27" (69cm) or desired length to ankle.

Heel:

Redistribute the sts so there are 15 sts on both sides of the marker on one needle and divide the remaining 32 sts (instep sts) on the other two needles.

Work back and forth over 30 heel sts in the following pattern:

Row 1 (WS): Sl 1, P28. Leave last, unworked st on right-hand needle. Turn work.

Row 2 (RS): Sl 1, K27. Leave unworked sts on right-hand needle. Turn work.

Row 3: Sl 1, P26. Turn work.

Row 4: Sl 1, K25. Turn work.

Continue working the heel as above until there are 11 unworked sts on both sides of the live sts. End on a WS row, turn work.

Next Row: K8, pick up strand between last knitted st and first unworked st, K together picked-up loop and first unworked st. Turn work.

Next Row: P9, pick up strand between last purled st and first unworked st, P together picked-up loop and first unworked st. Turn work.

Continue working the heel as above until all 30 heel sts are live. End with a purl row.

Foot:

Set Up Round 1: K to the marker (15 sts), remove marker. On new needle, K remaining heel sts, pick up and knit 4 sts between heel and instep sts (Needle A). K all instep sts (32 sts) onto a single needle (Needle B). Pick up and knit 4 sts between instep and heel sts, K across first 15 heel sts (Needle C). 70 sts total.

Set Up Round 2: K all sts.

Round 1: K to last 3 sts on Needle A, K2tog, K1. Knit across sts on Needle B. At beginning of Needle C, K1, Sl 1, K1, Psso, K remaining sts.

Round 2: K all sts.

Repeat Rounds 1 and 2 three more times. 62 sts remain.

Continue in stockinette stitch until foot measures 2" (5cm) less than desired length.

Toe:

Round 1: K to last 3 sts on Needle A, K2tog, K1. On Needle B, K1, Sl 1, K1, Psso, K to last 3 sts, K2tog, K1. On Needle C, K1, Sl 1, K1, Psso, K remaining sts.

Round 2: K all sts.

Repeat Rounds 1 and 2 twelve more times. 10 sts remain.

With Needle C, K 2 sts from Needle A, then 1 st from Needle B, so that there are 5 sts each on two needles. Cut yarn leaving a long tail. With tail threaded on a tapestry needle, weave toe closed (Kitchener st).

Weave in ends.

Left stocking:

Repeat for second stocking using Left Stocking Chart.

Finishing:

Block the stockings to shape with either a steam iron on the "silk" setting or an ordinary iron and a damp press cloth. Make sure the seam is lined up along the back of the leg.

Resizing:

Other sizes can be calculated using a formula found in *The Good Housekeeping Needlecraft Encyclopedia*, edited by Alice Carroll (Hearst Magazines, Inc., 1947). Another more detailed stocking formula (Hand Knit Hose by Donna Kenton) that shapes more closely to the leg using decreases as well as increases can be found at www.tinyurl.com/yo5ruf. Keep in mind that shaping will have to move from the center back seam to at least 1" (2.54cm) from both sides of the snake pattern then back to the seam again to keep from distorting the position of the lace pattern.

In order to multi-size the stockings, the back seam is used to center the lace pattern but be aware that you will have to occasionally count backwards on the graph when the seam disappears just to make sure things are in their right place. On shorter stockings the snake pattern should be started sooner or the snake will be way down at the ankle rather than on the calf.

How to resize, via *The Good Housekeeping Needlecraft Encyclopedia*:

Work a circular gauge swatch and measure sample. The amount of stretch will depend on how much negative ease you want for your stocking and how much your yarn will stretch and still look nice. Most stockings have at least 1" (2.54cm) of negative ease.

Measure circumference of thigh, calf and ankle, and desired length of stocking from thigh to ankle. Subtract 1" (2.54cm) from each measurement for negative ease.

Use your measurements to calculate the total number of sts needed.

Example:
Gauge: 6 sts = 1" (2.5cm), 10 rows = 1" (2.5cm)
Thigh: 20" (51cm) [20 × 6 = 120 sts]
Calf: 14" (36cm) [14 × 6 = 84 sts]
Ankle: 10" (26cm) [10 × 6 = 60 sts]

Use your measurements to calculate the total number of rows and decreases needed.

Example:
Length of stocking to top of heel: 24" (61cm)
Thigh to Calf: 14" (36cm) [14 × 10 = 140 rows];
120 sts for thigh and 84 sts for calf [120 − 84 = 36 sts less at calf; 36 divided by 2 = 18 decreases; 140 rows divided by 18 decreases = 7¾, or one set of decreases every 8 rows.] Repeat calculations to determine rows and sts between calf and ankle.

Heel shaping: Divide total sts by two. One-half of sts will be instep sts and will be placed on needle no. 2, the rest of the sts will be divided between needles 1 and 3 and will be used for heel. Heel sts should be worked until 1" (2.5cm) (calculate number of sts from st gauge) is left unworked in the center of the needle.

Hallowed Counsel

Picking up a strand of yarn between the worked and unworked stitches when turning a heel will prevent those holes that always show up when working short rows.

Rather than using the usual square Dutch heel, I've used a technique found in Alice Carroll's 1947 *Good Housekeeping Needlecraft Encyclopedia*. The auto-heel fits the foot smoothly and can be replaced as easily as the Dutch heel.

When a garment has negative ease, it is actually smaller than the body part it will be covering, and will stretch to conform to the curves it covers. Stockings and similar close-fitting items should have at least 1" (2.54cm) of negative ease for a close fit.

A larger-gauge yarn will require more unworked rows in heel and toe shaping. Toes will require at least 2" (5cm) of shaping, so calculate row decreases according to gauge.

Designer bio:

Severina is the stern corset-wearing alter-ego of designer Aundrea Murphy, who lives in a strange world cluttered with black silk, jet beads and Bakelite. She fantasizes about ruling the world with her steam-powered robot army and when she isn't doing that she obsesses on dusty old books, vinyl albums, photographs of people she doesn't know, and reproducing clothing using antique needlework and sewing patterns. Currently she wastes quite a bit of valuable bandwidth at vintagestitchorama.blogspot.com.

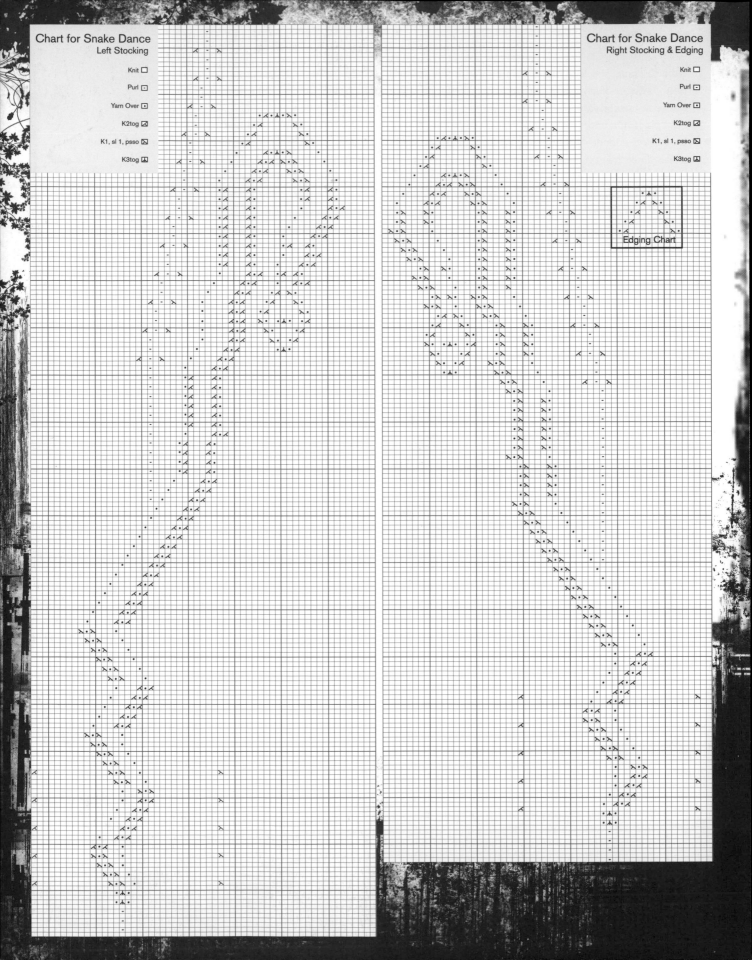

Chart for Snake Dance
Left Stocking

Knit ☐

Purl ⊡

Yarn Over ⊡

K2tog ◿

K1, sl 1, psso ◺

K3tog ◹

Chart for Snake Dance
Right Stocking & Edging

Knit ☐

Purl ⊡

Yarn Over ⊡

K2tog ◿

K1, sl 1, psso ◺

K3tog ◹

Edging Chart

antispeak

You don't think like anyone else you know, so why speak like them? Here are some of our favorite words to annoy friends and alienate stupid people:

Catharsis (ka-thar-sis) noun

A purging or cleansing that brings relief, very often done through artistic expression. *Carrie knew raining down hellfire and destruction on her classmates was petty, but damn it was cathartic!*

Chthonic (kuh-thon-ik) adj.

Very old and strong, slightly primal power, relating often to deities and energies beneath the earth. *Tiffani secretly adored going to the spa for a volcanic mud facial, not because it left her skin so soft, but because it appealed to something chthonic inside her.*

Limen (lim-en) noun

The edge where two areas overlap. *When ordering a refreshing drink in the astral plane, do not ask for a twist of limen.*

Obstreperous (aub-strep-er-us) adj.

Noisily defiant. *Silence those obstreperous children, for they are interfering with my cocktail hour!*

Quixotic (kwik-zot-ik) adj.

Foolishly impractical, often in pursuit of ideals. *We tried to tell Roger that making an igloo out of Jell-O in the middle of a heat wave was a quixotic pursuit, but he wouldn't listen.*

Schadenfreude (sha-den-froy-duh) noun

Taking delight in the misery of others. *Thanks to the Internet, you can now get your schadenfreude on 24/7.*

Seditious (seh-dih-shus) adj.

Relating to something or someone that incites riot or rebellion. *Seditious rhymes with Sid Vicious. Coincidence? We think not.*

Thaumaturgy (thau-ma-tur-gee) noun

Magic done using your own reservoir of power. *See Dick. See Dick run. See Dick use thaumaturgy to crush his enemies. Use thaumaturgy, Dick!*

17

GOTHIC GLAM YULE HAT

BY ERSSIE MAJOR

This is a hat for a seasonal festivity for all those who avoid the dreaded "C" word and prefer to call it Yuletide. Every discerning follower of Yule needs an antidote to the bright colors this season forces upon them. This luxurious pointy head gear could mean you are the envy of the choir whilst singing in darkened doorways on cold nights. However, it could also be the catalyst to launch your solo carol-singing career.

MOOD ENHANCERS:

"Chanukkah, Oh Chanukkah," *Excelsis* by Black Tape For a Blue Girl (OK, so it's not the "C" word originally referred to, but it's a damn cool song. C'mon, get your holiday multiculturalism on.)

SKILLS USED:

Basic knitting (see page 131)
Intarsia (see page 143)
Mattress Stitch (see page 142)

MATERIALS AND TOOLS:

2 balls (87 yards or 78 meters ea) Wendy Chic nylon/polyester blend yarn in color 250 Renoir
2 balls (71 yards or 64 meters ea) Debbie Bliss Alpaca Silk Aran baby alpaca/silk blend yarn in color 01 Black
1 ball (71 yards or 64 meters ea) or oddments Debbie Bliss Alpaca Silk Aran baby alpaca/silk blend yarn in color 02 Cream
1 ball (71 yards or 64 meters ea) or oddments Debbie Bliss Alpaca Silk Aran baby alpaca/silk blend yarn in color 19 Red
1 ball (71 yards or 64 meters ea) or oddments Debbie Bliss Alpaca Silk Aran baby alpaca/silk blend yarn in color 05 Pine
1 ball (71 yards or 64 meters ea) or oddments Debbie Bliss Alpaca Silk Aran baby alpaca/silk blend yarn in color 11 Claret
US #8 (5mm) straight or circular knitting needles (or size needed to obtain gauge)
US #7 (4.5mm) straight or circular knitting needles (or size .5mm smaller than larger needles)
Stitch markers
Tapestry needle

GAUGE:

17 sts × 24 rows = 4" (10cm) using alpaca silk on larger needles in stockinette stitch

FINISHED SIZE:

Sizing: Adult Small (Medium, Large)
Circumference: 19 (21, 22½)" (48 [53, 57]cm)

NOTES:

The hat is knitted flat with a simple Fair Isle detail and is seamed up the back. The elfin shape is achieved by paired decreases with plain rows between, gradually decreasing to the point, which is decorated with a pom-pom.

Hallowed Counsel

When knitting with black yarn, get a full-spectrum light bulb to help you see the individual stitches better. You can also cover your lap with a white sheet.

—Renée

9

Brim:

Using smaller needles and Wendy Chic, cast on 80 (88, 96) sts.
Work in 1×1 ribbing (K1, P1) for 4" (10cm), or desired length.

Motif:

Switch to larger needles and black Alpaca Silk.

Next Row (RS): K31 (35, 39), Pm, K19, Pm, K30 (34, 38).

Next Row (WS): P all sts, sl all markers.

Next Row (begin chart, page 21): K to marker, sl marker, work Row 1 of chart over next 19 sts, sl marker, K to end.

Next Row: P to marker, sl marker, work Row 2 of chart over next 19 sts, sl marker, P to end.

Continue as set in stockinette until all 20 rows of the chart have been worked.

Work 1 row even, removing markers as you come to them.

Get pointy (decreases):

Set Up Row (WS): P10 (11, 12), Pm, P20 (22, 24), Pm, P20 (22, 24), Pm, P20 (22, 24), Pm, P10 (11, 12).

Row 1: *K to 2 sts before marker, Ssk, sl marker, K2tog; repeat from * 3 times more, K to end.

Rows 2, 4, 6, 8, 10: P all sts, sl all markers.

Rows 3, 5, 7, 9: K all sts, sl all markers.

Repeat Rows 1–10 until 8 (12, 12) sts remain.

Cut yarn, draw through remaining sts, pull tight and fasten off.

Finishing:

Join the side edges together to form back seam using mattress stitch or other method of invisible seaming. Sew in ends. If desired, make a pom-pom and attach to the point of the hat.

How to Make a Pom-Pom

For a 3" (8cm) pom-pom, cut out two circles, 3" (8cm) in diameter from card stock. Cut out a smaller circle (approximately 1¼" (3cm) in diameter) from the center of each to make two donut-shaped rings. Stack the rings and wrap Wendy Chic yarn around the rings and through the center opening until the ring is full. Using scissors, cut through the wrapped yarn around the outside of the ring, slipping the blades between the two rings as a guide. When all the yarn has been cut, tie a piece of yarn around the yarn at the center of the ring between the two layers of card. Remove the cardboard rings and fluff the pom-pom to form a ball.

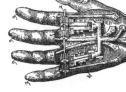

Designer bio:

Erssie Major has been knitting since a child, learning skills passed down the female line of a West Country family in the United Kingdom. As a tomboy who knits, one of her first designs included knitting, crocheting and sewing garments for her action soldier toy. (Picture a male doll with a beard in a flowery quilt set with a crocheted dressing gown!) After a long break from knitting and crocheting, she returned to the craft after a chronic illness and advocates knitting as therapy for anyone who is ill, disabled or suffers from depression. Erssie has been published online in The AntiCraft, MagKnits, and on The Children's Society website. She has also had designs published in *The Art of Knitting, Simply Knitting,* and *Yarn Forward.* She has contributed her designs, made items, and checked patterns for the book *Hookorama* and has contributed to other books either as a designer, maker, or technical editor. She is currently working on a book of her own.

You can find Erssie online at www.erssie .blogspot.com and www.erssieknits.com.

20

TOP 5 REASONS IT'S GOOD TO BE AN ANTICRAFTER

5 Laundry is so much easier to do when all your clothes are black.

4 It's fun to watch people do double takes when they ask what you are knitting and you reply in all seriousness, "A teratoma."

3 It makes family members shake their heads in sadness and disgust. They're so cute when they're dejected!

2 You're going to die anyway, so you might as well craft.

1 Until you master your coolness, your coolness will be your master.

BELLADONNA SLEEVES

BY ERSSIE MAJOR

This project was inspired by the Belladonna plant. Large bobbles glisten wickedly like the dark cherry-like fruit of this poisonous herb also known as Deadly Nightshade and the sleeves gently flare like the small purple fluted flowers. As well as providing an atropine for Venetian ladies to dilate their pupils, the poison has been combined with other fatal herbs to make a flying ointment that could put witches into a trance state close to death just by rubbing ointment onto their temples. It has been well recorded that on these occasions, a body can become uncommonly cold whilst the spirit is absent in another dimension and a lady has to have something in her handbag she can slip on her arms whilst in a strappy evening dress. The sleeves can also be worn under a T-shirt and are easily folded like gloves to pop in your bag for an evening out when a cardigan is just too bulky.

MOOD ENHANCERS:

"Belladonna," *Hyaena* by Siouxsie and the Banshees

SKILLS USED:

Basic knitting (see page 131)
Bobble (as explained in project instructions)

MATERIALS AND TOOLS:

2 balls (227 yards or 204 meters ea) Rowan Kidsilk Night kid mohair/silk/polyester/nylon blend yarn in color 614 Macbeth (Yarn A)
2 (3, 3) balls (103 yards or 93 meters ea) Rooster Almerino Aran baby alpaca/merino wool blend yarn in color 308 Spiced Plum (Yarn B)
1 reel (208 yards or 187 meters) of black knitting elastic for ribbing on upper arm (optional)
1 set 7mm double-point needles, or size needed to obtain gauge (the closest equivalent US size is US #10 [6mm])
1 set 7.5mm double-point needles, or size .5mm larger than smallest needles (the closest equivalent US size is US #10.5 [6.5mm])
1 set US #13 (9mm) double-point needles (or size 2mm larger than smallest needles)
Tapestry needle

GAUGE:

12.5 sts × 17 rows = 4" (10cm) in stockinette on smallest needles, using yarns A and B held together.

FINISHED SIZE:

Size: Small (Medium, Large)
Sleeve length: 17 (18, 18½)" (43 [46, 47]cm)
Wrist to upper ribbing length: 12 (13, 13)" (30 [33, 33]cm)
Upper ribbing length: 3½ (3½, 4)" (9 [9, 10cm)
Wrist circumference: 6 (6½, 7½)" (16 [17, 19]cm)
See *Resizing* at the end of the pattern to learn how to calculate a custom fit.

SPECIAL STITCHES:

Make Bobble (MD)

Row 1: K1, Yo, K1, Yo, K1 into the same st. Turn work.
Row 2: P5. Turn work.
Row 3: K5. Turn work.
Row 4: P2tog, P1, P2tog. Turn work.
Row 5: Sl1 Kwise, K2tog, Psso.

NOTES:

Due to the large gauge of the knit, only one stitch is increased at the end of the round on the underside of the arm, instead of the traditional two increases per round. All increased stitches should be incorporated into the established ribbing pattern. To avoid complicating the pattern, some changes to the needle sizes are made in order to shape and open up the top part of the ribbing for the width of the upper arm.

Cuff:

Using both yarns held together and smallest double-point needles cast on 45 (45, 54) sts. Pm and join together in a round without twisting the stitches.

Rounds 1–3: (K4, P5) around.

Round 4: (K4, P2tog, P3) around. 40 (40, 48) sts remain.

Rounds 5–7: (K4, P4) around.

Round 8: (K4, P2tog, P2) around. 35 (35, 42) sts remain.

Rounds 9–11: (K4, P3) around.

Round 12: (K4, P2tog, P1) around. 30 (30, 36) sts remain.

Rounds 13–15: K4, P2 around.

Round 16: (K4, P2tog) around. 25 (25, 30) sts remain.

Round 17: (K4, P1) around.

Round 18: (K3, K2tog) around. 20 (20, 24) sts remain.

Small and Medium sizes:

Rounds 19–21: K all sts. 20 (20) sts remain.

Large size only:

Rounds 19–20: K all sts.

Round 21: K to end of round, M1. 25 sts remain.

Wrist to Top of Arm:

Set Up Rounds: (K2, P3) around for three rounds.

Round 1 (Bobble rnd A): [K2, P3, K2, P1, MB, P1] twice, work remaining sts in K2, P3 ribbing pattern.

Round 2 (Inc rnd): (K2, P3) to end of round, M1. 21 (21, 26) sts remain.

Rounds 3–4: work all sts in K2, P3 ribbing.

Round 5 (Bobble rnd B): [K2, P1, MB, P1, K2, P3], twice, work remaining sts in K2, P3 ribbing.

Round 6: same as Round 2.

Rounds 7–8: same as Round 3.

Small size only:

Repeat Rounds 1–8 four more times, then Rounds 1–4 once, eliminating the increase in Round 2. 30 sts remain.

Medium and Large sizes:

Repeat Rounds 1–8 three more times. Repeat Rounds 1–8 again, but increase two sts in Round 6 instead of one.

Repeat Rounds 1–8 once more, but increase 2 sts at end of Rounds 2 and 6. 35 (40) sts.

All sizes:

Next Round: Switch to 7.5mm double-point needles. (K2, P2tog, P1) around. 24 (28, 32) sts remain.

Upper Ribbing:

Continue on with 7.5mm double-point needles, holding knitting elastic together with the yarns if desired. Work in 2×2 ribbing (K2, P2) for 3½ (3½, 4)" (9 [9, 10]cm).

Switch to US #13 (9mm) double-point needles, work one additional round of 2×2 ribbing (K2, P2).

Bind off loosely. Sew in ends.

Finishing:

Block lightly if needed.

Resizing:

Measure your arm from wrist to underarm. Then measure your wrist circumference. Cast on the correct number of stitches to obtain correct wrist circumference and adjust the length at the upper arm by continuing the repeat pattern for as long as desired or adding a wider welt of ribbing. The fit of these sleeves is very forgiving as the rib will expand and contract giving a good leeway.

Designer bio:

To read about Erssie, see page 20.

Hallowed Counsel

If the Deadly Nightshade colorway is too dangerous for comfort, why not try Rooster Almerino Gooseberry with GGH Soft Kid mohair. However, even gooseberries consumed to excess can give rise to symptoms of poisoning.

POP ART SKULLS

BY ERSSIE MAJOR

Growing up I just about devoured anything that emerged from Andy Warhol's "The Factory," especially the prolific screen prints of American pop culture. Obviously the bright shapes against a luminous background and the unit-based repetition of the motifs on this pillow are more than a passing nod in Warhol's direction.

MOOD ENHANCERS:

"Walk on the Wild Side," *Transformer* by Lou Reed

SKILLS USED:

Basic knitting (see page 131)

Intarsia (see page 143)

Duplicate stitch (optional; see page 144)

MATERIALS AND TOOLS:

4 skeins (114 yards or 103 meters ea) Texere Yarns Chunky Wool 100% wool yarn in color #5 Grass (MC)

1 skein (114 yards or 103 meters ea) Texere Yarns Chunky Wool 100% wool yarn in color #16 Cerise

1 skein (114 yards or 103 meters ea) Texere Yarns Chunky Wool 100% wool yarn in color #4 Turquoise

1 skein (114 yards or 103 meters ea) Texere Yarns Chunky Wool 100% wool yarn in color #10 Sunshine

1 skein (114 yards or 103 meters ea) Texere Yarns Chunky Wool 100% wool yarn in color #6 Emerald

1 skein (114 or 103 meters yards ea) Texere Yarns Chunky Wool 100% wool yarn in color #2 Royal

US #8 (5mm) straight or circular knitting needles (or size needed to obtain gauge)

sewing machine for seaming OR tapestry needle

18" × 18" (46cm × 46cm) pillow form or foam rubber cut to size

GAUGE:

18 sts × 20 rows = 4" (10cm) in stockinette

FINISHED SIZE:

18" × 18" (46cm x 46cm)

NOTES:

The Texere yarn knits up very firmly at this gauge, which will give you a more durable pillow sham.

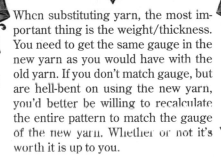

Hallowed Counsel

When substituting yarn, the most important thing is the weight/thickness. You need to get the same gauge in the new yarn as you would have with the old yarn. If you don't match gauge, but are hell-bent on using the new yarn, you'd better be willing to recalculate the entire pattern to match the gauge of the new yarn. Whether or not it's worth it is up to you.

—Erssie Major

The skull on each circle can be worked as an intarsia or Fair Isle motif as the cushion is knit. Or, if you fancy making more time to lounge around on this pillow, you could choose to knit only the circles in intarsia, leaving the skull motifs to be worked in duplicate stitch.

Front:

Cast on 83 sts in MC.

P one row.

Work all rows of Pop Art Skulls Cushion Chart, starting at the bottom right-hand corner.

K one row.

Bind off all sts.

Back (A):

Cast on 83 sts in MC.

Work in stockinette stitch for 8" (20cm).

Work in 2×2 ribbing (K2, P2) for 1" (2.5cm).

Bind off all sts.

Back (B):

Cast on 83 sts in MC.

Work flat in stockinette stitch for 11½" (29cm).

Work in 2×2 ribbing (K2, P2) for 1" (2.5cm).

Bind off all sts.

Assembling and finishing:

Block all pieces. Place Front face up, lay and pin Back (A) face down over the top part of Front, and Back (B) face down over the bottom part of Front, so that ribbed edges on Back (A) and (B) overlap at the center of the cushion. Stitch all pieces together using an elastic stitch (zigzag or a stitch designed for stretch fabrics) on a machine capable of coping with knit fabrics.

If you'd prefer not to use a sewing machine, sew all pieces together by hand, making sure the seam goes through both back pieces where they overlap. Stuff with pillow form or piece of foam rubber cut to size.

Designer bio:

To read about Erssie, see page 20.

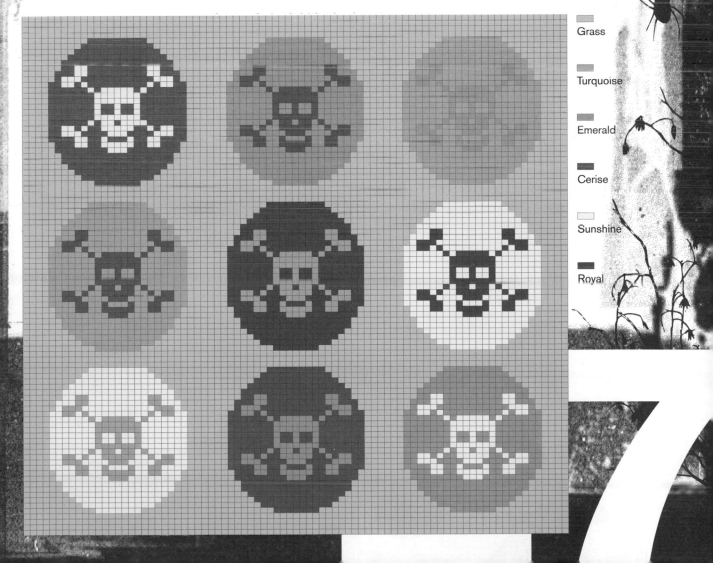

Grass

Turquoise

Emerald

Cerise

Sunshine

Royal

What's your perfect lair?

Home is where the heart is, even if your heart is a shriveled up, black walnut-like thing. Home is where you can relax and be yourself, so it's very important to find yourself a lair that reflects who you are and what you value. Sound daunting? Don't you worry—our Quiz-o-Matic Lair Finder does all the work for you!

Answer the questions and make a note of how many points your answer is worth. At the end, total your points to be placed in your perfect lair.

1. When faced with cobwebs so thick they obscure the passageway beyond, you think:

A. Aw, isn't it a precious arachnid? Yes it is! (1 pt)

B. Bats would probably eat spiders, wouldn't they? Good source of protein. (5 pts)

C. I wonder if that's a violation of the local housing code? (2 pts)

D. It's time to sack the maid, if I can find her. Haven't seen her in a while, come to think of it. Or the butler. (4 pts)

E. No problem, my trip-hop beats will send any spiders scurrying in no time. (3 pts)

2. If the previous owners still visit, they are:

A. Really pale with pointy teeth. (5 pts)

B. Rednecks. (2 pts)

C. Skeletons taken apart and made into chandeliers and candlesticks. (1 pt)

D. Sort of shimmery and transparent. (4 pts)

E. Wanted for tax evasion. (3 pts)

3. Your favorite color is:

A. Black, black, black. (1 pt)

B. Blood red. (5 pts)

C. Does "strobe light" count as a color? (3 pts)

D. Ichor green. (4 pts)

E. Violet. (2 pts)

4. Your ideal mode of transportation is:

A. A hearse. (1 pt)

B. A stagecoach pulled by four black horses. (4 pts)

C. An old car covered in obscure and/or obscene bumper stickers. (2 pts)

D. Public—I'm an urbanite and proud of it. (3 pts)

E. The night wind. And maybe a ship. (5 pts)

5. Which of these building materials calls to you the most?

A. Brick. (4 pts)

B. Stainless steel. (3 pts)

C. Stone. (5 pts)

D. Tin. (2 pts)

E. Wood. (1 pt)

6. Which of these fabrics calls to you the most?

A. Anything, so long as it's tattered and moldy. (1 pt)

B. Heavy silk. (4 pts)

C. Latex. (3 pts)

D. Velvet. (2 pts)

E. Woven tapestry. (5 pts)

7. Which of the following would you NOT be caught dead in?

A. A necklace of garlic. (5 pts)

B. Anything that might get stained by my candy necklace. (3 pts)

C. Clothing of any kind—while sitting at the computer anyway. (2 pts)

D. I'm already dead, so this question doesn't really apply to me. (1 pt)

E. Anything lacking a ruff, cravat, corset, or overcoat. (4 pts)

8. Your coffee is:

A. Black, black, black. (1 pt)

B. Cuban. (2 pts)

C. I don't drink . . . coffee. (5 pts)

D. Look, it doesn't HAVE to be from Starbucks, it's just that there's one on my way home and it's not like their coffee is BAD, and as far as soul-crushing giant companies go they really are the best of the bunch, very eco-friendly and working-mom friendly . . . ! (3 pts)

E. Tea, actually. With milk and sugar. (4 pts)

9. Your favorite or ideal kind of pet is:

A. Cat. (2 pts)

B. Please, I kill plants, the last thing I need is a pet. (3 pts)

C. Rat. (1 pt)

D. Will 'o wisp. (4 pts)

E. Wolf. (5 pts)

10. Your favorite author is:

A. Bram Stoker. (5 pts)

B. It's too dark in here to read. (1 pt)

C. Poppy Z. Brite. (3 pts)

D. Edgar Allen Poe. (4 pts)

E. Them folks at *The Weekly World News.* (2 pts)

If you scored:

10–15 points

You, my dear, are a Crypt dweller. It's likely you're already dead and in a box, or maybe you're just striving too hard to be waif-chic. You like the dark and the creepy crawlies—modern conveniences be damned! Your life (or death) isn't a whirlwind of excitement, but that's OK with you. You're laid back (or laid to rest) enough to appreciate the set-in-stone décor and lack of natural light.

16–25 points

Funky as you may be, your lust for a purple velvet chaise lounge that the previous owners left will seal the deal and turn you into a Mobile Home-owning upright citizen. Let's just hope it's a double-wide, shall we? Never fear, we are confident that your inherent funkiness will prevail and you'll be able to turn that trailer into the mobile lair of your dreams. Perhaps you can locate a local Crypt dweller to lend you some of his or her spiders?

26–35 points

The lair for you, our LARPing urban fiend, is the sought-after Converted Abandoned Warehouse. You have the most space, and therefore your lair is the place to be for parties. Your need to impress far outweighs your anti-social nature, but having these two conflicting desires means there will always be drama-fodder on hand. Just don't be surprised if your dancetastic strobe light system gives a few of your guests seizures.

36–45 points

Your blue-blood inbreeding leaves you with social skills that are so lacking you really only interact well with the dead, and you've seen *Poltergiest* like a gazillion times, so you're more than comfortable living in a giant Haunted Mansion. While danger of possession or running into a deadly curse is high, the Haunted Mansion at least already comes furnished and with a full staff of the undead that you won't have to worry about paying.

46 points or more

You're a traditionalist. You like your blood to be red, your hotties to be pale, and your dwelling to be a big Stone Castle, replete with creepy full moon backdrop, fog machines, and howling wolves soundtrack. It's killing you that Anne Rice has decided to write about Jesus, but your heart is so old and dry that you can no longer woop—or so you tell everyone on your MySpace page.

29

TOUGH BABY

BY SABRINA THOMPSON

Sweater, n: garment worn by child when its mother is feeling chilly. —Ambrose Bierce, American writer, journalist, editor, 1842-1914

Two things have inspired the design of this sweater: First, I had a ball each of blue, purple, and black yarn that I needed to use up to make room in my knitting basket. Second, and probably more important than the first, was inspired by my going out and shopping for some pregnant friends of mine and tired of seeing the typical pastel-and-cartoon-sugar-coated baby clothes that exist. I wanted to see something with a little more attitude. Unable to find it, I created it.

MOOD ENHANCERS:

The Nightmare Before Christmas (1993, rated PG)

SKILLS USED:

Basic knitting (see page 131)
Intarsia (see page 143)
Pick up stitches (see page 140)
Mattress stitch (see page 142)

MATERIALS AND TOOLS:

1 ball (200 yards or 180 meters) Patons Canadiana acrylic yarn color 00003 Black (MC)
1 ball (200 yards or 180 meters) Patons Canadiana acrylic yarn color 00032 Bright Royal Blue (CC1)
1 ball (195 yards or 176 meters) Bernat Berella 4 acrylic yarn color 00724 Velvet Night (CC2)
US #8 (5mm) straight or circular knitting needles (or size needed to obtain gauge)
US #8 (5mm) 12" (30cm) or 16" (41cm) circular knitting needle (or size needed to obtain gauge)
1 set US #8 (5mm) double-point needles (or size needed to obtain gauge)
2 stitch holders
Tapestry needle

GAUGE:

18 sts × 24 rows = 4" (10cm) in stockinette

FINISHED SIZE:

Size: 18 months
Chest: 26" (66cm)
Length: 12" (30cm)
Sleeve length: 7" (18cm)
Neck: 6" (15cm) wide
Shoulder (neck to sleeve): 3.5" (9cm)

Hallowed Counsel

One of the more foolproof methods of checking to see if a new yarn is a suitable substitute is to measure Wraps per Inch (WPI). A WPI tool can be bought for about ten dollars and they are widely available online. You simply wrap the original yarn around the tool, which is marked in inches like a ruler, and count how many wraps per inch that yarn has. You then do the same for the new yarn. If the WPI match, it means the yarns are interchangeable weight/thickness-wise and should yield the same gauge when knit up. (Always swatch!) You can then use the new yarn without having to recalculate any of the pattern.

—Zabet

Back:

Cast on 54 sts in MC.

Work in 1×1 ribbing (K1, P1) for two rows.

Work in stockinette stitch in the stripe pattern below.

Stripe pattern: 3 rows MC, 2 rows CC1, 2 rows MC, 2 rows CC1, 2 rows MC, 2 rows CC1, 2 rows MC, 4 rows CC2, 2 rows MC, 2 rows CC1, 2 rows MC, 2 rows CC1, 2 rows MC, 4 rows CC1, 2 rows MC, 2 rows CC1, 2 rows MC, 4 rows CC2, 2 rows MC, 2 rows CC1, 2 rows MC, 4 rows CC1. End on a WS row. Piece should measure about 11" (28cm).

Next row (MC): BO 7 sts, K remaining sts. Turn work.

Next row (MC): BO 7 sts, P remaining sts. Turn work.

Next row (CC1): BO 7 sts, K remaining sts. Turn work.

Next row (CC1): BO 7 sts, P remaining sts. Turn work.

Work in stockinette stitch in MC for 2 rows over remaining 26 sts. Place remaining sts on a stitch holder.

Front:

Cast on 54 sts in MC.

Work in 1×1 ribbing (K1, P1) for two rows.

Work in stockinette stitch, randomly adding skull motif in CC1 and CC2, until piece measures 9" (23cm). End with a WS row.

Next row (RS): K20, place remaining sts on stitch holder. Turn work.

Shoulder row 1: P2tog, P to end of row. Turn work.

Shoulder row 2: K to last 2 sts, K2tog. Turn work.

Repeat Shoulder rows 1 and 2 two more times. 14 sts remain.

Continue in stockinette stitch until work measures 11" (28cm).

Next row: BO 7 sts, K remaining sts. Turn work.

Next row: P7. Turn work.

Bind off sts.

Replace 20 sts of left shoulder on needle, leaving 14 center sts on stitch holder. Join MC and work left shoulder as for right shoulder, reversing shaping.

Collar:

Sew together the two shoulder seams with mattress stitch. With circular needle and CC2, pick up 14 sts from front stitch holder, then 9 sts around right front neck edge, 26 sts from back stitch holder, then 9 sts around left neck edge. 58 sts.

Work in 1×1 ribbing (K1, P1) for 1 round.

Bind off all sts in pattern.

Sleeves:

Sew front and back pieces together at the side with mattress stitch. Start at the bottom of the sweater and seam to 5" (13cm) from the shoulder, leaving an opening for the sleeves. Pick up 39 sts evenly on double-point needles around the sleeve opening. Work stockinette stitch in the round until the sleeve measures 6" (15cm). Switch yarns while knitting for striped sleeves, if you desire.

Next row: K2tog, K remaining sts. 38 sts remain.

Switch to contrast color, if you desire. Work in stockinette stitch for an additional 1" (2.5cm).

Work in 1×1 ribbing (K1, P1) for 1 round.

Bind off all sts in pattern.

Repeat for second sleeve.

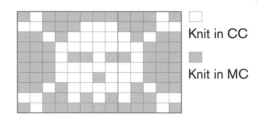

☐ Knit in CC

▨ Knit in MC

Designer bio:

My knitting and I live in Mississauga, Ontario, Canada, with my darling husband and adoptive joint-custody kitty, who both find themselves tangled in my current projects. When I can manage to get my head out of my knitting basket, my free time is filled with taking road trips with my car-obsessed husband, dreaming of moving to the desert, untangling myself from my overgrown garden, and mastering the art of cooking without burning.

Cheesy Lentil Bake—The Only Thing Cheesier Than This Dish Is Its Name

12 oz dry red lentils
3 cups filtered water
2 teaspoons salt
black pepper to taste
½ teaspoon cayenne pepper (ground red pepper)
4 tablespoons chili powder
2 zucchini, peeled and minced
3 medium-large onions, chopped
3 cups cheddar cheese, shredded
2 eggs

Rinse lentils until water runs clear (this will take 3-5 times). Put lentils, water, and spices into a heavy saucepan. Bring to a boil and reduce heat to a simmer. Simmer for 15-20 minutes until all water is absorbed. Let cool completely.

Preheat oven to 375ºF. In a large mixing bowl, combine cooled lentils, vegetables, and cheese. In a smaller bowl, beat eggs. Add eggs to larger bowl and mix well. Put mixture in a greased 4 qt. glass casserole dish. Bake 55-60 minutes.

(This recipe is based on Meg Pickard's Cheese and Lentil Loaf, which itself was based on a recipe from Sarah Brown's *Vegetarian Kitchen*.)

Makes 12 servings. Can be halved.

Succulent Black Bean Stew

1 small onion, chopped
2 cloves of garlic, smashed
cooking spray
1 scallion, snipped into bits
1 can organic black beans, rinsed and drained
½ cup fat free chicken broth
1 small peach, peeled, pitted, and chopped
Cajun seasoning, cayenne pepper, and hot sauce to taste

Coat a nonstick skillet with cooking spray and heat. Sauté the onion and garlic until the onion is softened and fragrant. Add scallion, beans, broth, peach, and spices to the skillet. Bring to a boil, then reduce heat and simmer until liquid has mostly evaporated. Adjust seasoning if desired.

Makes 2 hearty servings.

Rock the Cradle of Love:

PARENTING FROM THE DARK SIDE OF THE MOON

You only get one chance to raise the perfect kid. The odds are against you on that one, but the good news is there are infinite chances to screw them up. With your luck, your children are going to grow up to be fine, upstanding, khaki-wearing, SUV-driving, milk-drinking adults. That's how kids are. They rebel. But while they are infants and toddlers, you can bend them to your will for that short period of time. Here's how.

Paint It Black

Ah, the nursery. A place of sunshine and light, a place for your dear sweet schnookums to rest his pretty little head. If teddy bears and nonironic unicorns irritate you, how do you think your helpless infant feels about these things? Just because he cannot talk does not mean that he should have to endure—shudder—cuteness.

Consider your own tastes when decorating the nursery for the coming (or already here, if you're a procrastinator) bundle of sleepless nights and endless diapers—or, joy, bundle of joy. Do you like pretty, pretty princesses? No? Then your child won't either. If, however, you like reproductions of pulp fiction covers and mysterious thrift store finds, you and your baby have found a theme you can both live with. Don't be afraid to really go for it. Babies need visual stimulation, after all. Consider a mobile of shrunken heads. Why not?

Ga Ga. Gah!

Baby talk is neither energy efficient, nor is it AntiCraftastic. If someone came up to you and said, "Oh aren't you dark and scary? Who's dark and scary? Oh you are, you creepy little thing you," you would at the very least give them the icy stare of death. Should your child be forced to endure this because they have not mastered their very own icy stare of death? We say no! Talk to your child as though your child were a real live person. She may seem like a squirming, eating, and pooping monster right now, but one day she will talk. If you want her to be able to talk down to others, you have to talk up to her now.

Sweet Lullaby

Rock a bye baby, in the tree top,
When the bough breaks, the cradle will drop.

What's with that? Does your child really need to fear that you will drop her from a tree? The children's songs that are not mindnumbingly repetitive are violent and cruel. Why not choose music that both you and your child can enjoy listening to. Give her the chance, and soon she'll be singing "The Tiny Goat" by the Gothic Archies rather than some insipid song about crushing up baby bumble bees. Sure, they are both sad and an animal dies in each, but one has a good beat, and the other makes you want to beat yourself in the head with a mallet.

Why Cloth Is Goth

Does spending all your absinthe money on covering your child's bum with mainstream cartoon characters seem like a good idea? If so, disposable diapers are the way to go. But if you are reading this book, you probably honor both your alcohol and your sinister crafting skills. If so, you are a prime subject to make your own cloth diapers. There are work-at-home parents out there who will make them for you—think endlessly customizable—or you can follow one of the many patterns available on the Internet.

Babies—Not Billboards

Your child did not ask to be an advertisement for the local mall. Children do not care about what's "in" this season, and you probably don't either. That said, why not dress your children in something that will really stand out in a crowd? Plain onesies are cheap, and so is fabric paint, so bust out some cardstock and make some stencils. Suggested subjects for your stencils might include skulls (it's never too early for skulls), aliens, and—of course—wheelbarrows.

Arts and AntiCrafts

Coloring books are stupid and gender biased, so why not let your future NEA grant reject redefine the look of your home with crayons. Or sharpies. Or shoe polish. Just choose colors that match your décor—black should feature heavily here—and you will have one-of-a-kind murals (up to and including two and a half feet from the floor) everywhere you look.

Feed Me, Seymour

Let's say you craft for fun. Just for giggles, because we are sure you picked up this book for the parenting advice. Crafts are expensive. Baby food is expensive. So either you are forced to lead a life without creativity, or your baby has to survive on ramen noodles. No more! Make your own baby food by pureeing cooked fruits and vegetables (there are websites that can be more specific if you search for them) and voilà! You've got baby food! It's cheaper and fresher, and there are no bizarre additives.

Finally, a Note on Hair

Whether you squeeze out a baby with a full head of hair or one as bald as Rob Halford, bows are unacceptable. If he has hair, consider a faux-hawk. If she is bald, consider temporary tattoos. Or rather, don't, because we don't know if that is safe. Let your bald baby be who she is, bald and allegedly responsible for driving teenage boys to suicide.

SKYLLA

BY DALE HWANG

It's a menstrual cup cozy shaped like a squid! Every menstrual cup deserves a finely crafted bag to keep it clean between cycles. This one is equally at home in a handbag, carried by itself, left hanging off a bathroom doorknob, or sitting on a shelf in full view.

This small drawstring bag is knit in one piece using double knitting and circular knitting techniques. It is fully lined, is roomy enough to also fit a cloth liner, and has a built in tentacle handle. Or, if you are not a convert to menstrual cups, use it as a tampon cozy instead. It is easily made longer for applicator tampons. It is also just the right size to keep a cell phone warm instead.

MOOD ENHANCERS:

Twenty Thousand Leagues Under the Sea by Jules Verne (www.gutenberg.org/etext/164); *The Odyssey* by Homer (www.gutenberg.org/etext/1727)

SKILLS USED:

Basic knitting (see page 131)
Advanced increases (as explained
in project instructions—optional)
Knitting in the round (see page 143)
Basic sewing

MATERIALS AND TOOLS:

1 ball (109 yards or 98 meters) Elann Sierra Aran wool/alpaca
color 717 Oak or 0790 Hyacinth
1 set US #5 (3.75mm) double-point needles
(or size needed to obtain gauge)
Stitch marker
Tapestry needle
2 white or pearl four-hole buttons
1 clear two-hole button (optional)
Black yarn or embroidery floss
Sewing needle
7" × 14" (18cm × 36cm) piece of fabric
with matching thread
Pins
Safety pin or bodkin
Iron
Sewing machine (optional)

GAUGE:

23 sts × 31 rows = 4" (10cm) in stockinette

SPECIAL STITCHES:

Make Bobble (MB)

Row 1: K1, Yo, K1, Yo, K1 into the same st. Turn work.

Row 2: P5. Turn work.

Row 3: K5. Turn work.

Row 4: P2tog, P1, P2tog. Turn work.

Row 5: Sl1 K-wise, K2tog, Psso.

Increase 1 stitch (inc1)

Lift the left leg of the stitch below the one just worked (not the one directly below the new stitch on the needle, but the stitch below it), twist it to the right so it forms a closed loop and knit into it. Alternately, any other increase which does not leave a hole may be worked.

Knit into stitch below (K1 below, Sl top st)

Knit into the stitch below the next stitch but do not drop the stitch above; holding the yarn in front, slip the stitch above purlwise. Return the yarn to the back to work the next stitch. This prevents the yarn from being caught behind the slipped stitch, forming an unsightly bar on the reverse side, and preventing the two stitches from separating at the top.

Double knitting (K1, Sl1)

Knit 1, then, with the yarn in front of the next stitch, slip 1 purlwise. Bring the yarn to the back to work the next stitch. This is one method of double knitting and forms an open tube that will permit the bottom of the squid to open up later. All sl1 in the body of the squid should be worked purlwise with the yarn in front of the slipped stitch.

Double knit increase (KSI inc)

This increase maintains the double knitting pattern of (K1, Sl1) when worked on both sides. To work it, (K1, Sl1) as before and then work an inc1 into the knit stitch of the (K1, Sl1) pair, ignoring the Sl1. Alternately, any other increase that does not leave a hole may be worked, just make sure the increase does not bind up the slipped stitch.

Centered double decrease (Sl2 kwise, K1, psso)

Slip 2 stitches at the same time knitwise, then knit 1 stitch. Pass the 2 slipped stitches over the 1 knit stitch.

I-cord

Knit all stitches in the row. Without turning, push the finished row to the other end of the double-point needle and knit across all stitches again. This forms a small, hollow tube. Repeat until I-cord reaches desired length.

Squid:

Cast on 3 sts.

Row 1: Sl1, K2.

Row 2: Sl1, M1, (K1 below, Sl top st), M1, K1.

Row 3: Sl1, K1, (K1, Sl1), K2.

Row 4: Sl1, M1, (K1 below, Sl top st), (K1, Sl1), (K1 below, Sl top st), M1, K1.

Row 5: Sl1, K1, (K1, Sl1)×3, K2.

Row 6: Sl1, M1, K1, (K1, Sl1)×3, K1, M1, K1.

Row 7: Sl1, K2, (K1, Sl1)×3, K3.

Row 8: Sl1, M1, K1, (K1 below, Sl top st), (K1, Sl1), (K1 below, Sl top st), K1, M1, K1.

Row 9: Sl1, K2, (K1, Sl1)×5, K3.

Row 10: Sl1, M1, K2, (K1, Sl1)×5, K2, M1, K1.

Row 11: Sl1, K3, (K1, Sl1)×5, K4.

Row 12: Sl1, M1, K2, (K1 below, Sl top st), (K1, Sl1)×5, (K1 below, Sl top st), K2, M1, K1.

Row 13: Sl1, K3, (K1, Sl1)×7, K4.

Row 14: Sl1, M1, K3, (K1, Sl1)×7, K3, M1, K1.

Row 15: Sl1, K4, (K1, Sl1)×7, K5.

Row 16: Sl1, SSK, K2, (K1, Sl1)×2, (KSI inc), (K1, Sl1)×3, (KSI inc), (K1, Sl1)×2, K2, K2tog, K1.

Row 17: Sl1, K3, (K1, Sl1) ×2, (KSI inc), Sl1, (K1, Sl1)×3, (KSI inc), Sl1, (K1, Sl1)×2, K4.

Rows 18–19: Sl1, K3, (K1, Sl1)×9, K4.

Row 20: Sl1, SSK, K1, (K1, Sl1)×3, (KSI inc), (K1, Sl1)×3, (KSI inc), (K1, Sl1)×3, K1, K2tog, K1.

Row 21: Sl1, K2, (K1, Sl1)×3, (KSI inc), Sl1, (K1, Sl1)×3, (KSI inc), Sl1, (K1, Sl1)×3, K3.

Rows 22–23: Sl1, K2, (K1, Sl1)×11, K3.

Row 24: Sl1, SSK, (K1, Sl1)×3, (KSI inc), (K1, Sl1)×5, (KSI inc), (K1, Sl1)×3, K2tog, K1.

Row 25: Sl1, K1, (K1, Sl1)×3, (KSI inc), Sl1, (K1, Sl1)×5, (KSI inc), Sl1, (K1, Sl1)×3, K2.

Rows 26–27: Sl1, K1, (K1, Sl1)×13, K2.

Row 28: SSK, (K1, Sl1)×3, (KSI inc), (K1, Sl1)×7, (KSI inc), (K1, Sl1)×3, K2tog.

Row 29: Sl1, (K1, Sl1)×3, (KSI inc), Sl1, (K1, Sl1)×7, (KSI inc), Sl1, (K1, Sl1)×3, K1.

Rows 30–31: Sl1, (K1, Sl1)×15, K1.

While working Round 32, place the slipped sts onto a separate needle from the K sts. Begin working in the round by knitting those slipped stitches off of their holding needle starting at *.

Round 32: Sl1, Pm, (K1,Sl1)×8, add another needle, (K1, Sl1)×7, K1, *, K17. 32 sts remain.

Round 33: K all sts.

Round 34: K3, inc1, K15, inc1, K14. 34 sts remain.

Round 35: K all sts.

Round 36: K12, inc1, K17, inc1, K5. 36 sts remain.

Round 37: K all sts.

Repeat Round 37 until work measures 4¼" (11cm) long (or ½" (1cm) longer than whatever needs to fit inside). Bind off all sts.

On the inside edge of the bound off squid (the purl side), count 2 rows down and pick up 36 sts around (knit-wise) in the purl bar of the stitches in the 2nd row, being sure to place the start of the row in the same place as before. Work in stockinette stitch for an additional ¾" (2cm).

Next round: (K4, K2tog)×6. 30 sts remain.

Next round: K all sts.

Begin tentacles:

There are ten tentacles: eight small tentacles that come to a point and are purely decorative and two long feeding tentacles that end in a flat portion and can be utilized as carry straps. They are all made from I-cord and all begin with three stitches. Rearrange the body stitches on the needles so two needles are free for working the I-cord.

Feeding tentacle 1:

Slip the last 2 sts of the round onto the working needle. Knit the first st of the round and then cast on 2 additional sts. Work these 5 sts as I-cord. Periodically tugging on the bottom of the I-cord helps even out its shape. Tug on it a bit before measuring the length. When the tentacle is 5" (13cm) long, or desired length, begin working flat.

Row 1: Sl1, K4. Turn work.

Row 2: Sl1, M1, K3, M1, K1. Turn work.

Rows 3–7: Sl1, K6. Turn work.

Row 8: Sl1, Ssk, K1, K2tog, K1. Turn work.

Row 9: Sl1, K4. Turn work.

Row 10: Sl1, (Sl2 kwise, K1, psso), K1. Turn work.

Row 11: Sl2 kwise, K1, psso.

Cut yarn and pull end through remaining st.

Small tentacles 1–4:

Slip the next 3 sts onto the working needle, backwards loop cast on 1 more st. Work these 4 sts as I-cord until the tentacle measures 2½" (6cm) long. Without turning, K2tog twice. Again, without turning, K2tog once more. Cut yarn and pull end through remaining st. Repeat for 3 more tentacles.

Feeding tentacle 2:

Work as for Feeding tentacle 1, beginning with the next 3 sts. The tentacle may be worked identically from the first and hook/loop tape or snaps can be sewn to the tentacles later, or they may simply be sewn together for a permanent strap. For a button closure, work a buttonhole on Row 5.

Row 5 (Buttonhole): Sl1, K2, yo, K2tog, K2.

Small tentacles 5–8:

Work as for Small tentacles 1–4.

Finishing:

Weave in all the ends. Wash and lightly block the squid.

Once the squid is dry, sew the eyes to both sides of the head, slightly lower than the mid-line of the feeding tentacles. Sew the desired fastener to the feeding tentacle(s). If using a button, sew it on with the knitting yarn, and fashion a shank if it does not have one.

Lining:

Photocopy the template and adjust the length if necessary to fit your squid. To do so, cut the template between the parallel lines and separate the pieces so the adjusted template is 1¾" (4cm) longer than the body of the squid (from the point to where the tentacles divide). To make the squid shorter, fold at the parallel lines instead.

Bias cut two pieces of fabric to match the adjusted template. The diagonal line on the template should be parallel to the selvedge.

With the wrong side out on the fabric, seam the lining together and baste together the top as marked on the template. Clip the fabric as marked and press the seams back. Remove the basting thread. Fold the top edge down and press flat, and repeat, as indicated on the template (the top ¼" (6mm), and then the next ½" (13mm). Stitch through all three layers ⅛" (3mm) from the first fold, creating a sleeve for the drawstring. Repeat for the other side.

Place the lining on the inside of the squid so the seam is centered under the feeding tentacles, and the top corners frame either tentacle's three stitches. Line up the top edge of the lining to just below where the tentacles begin. Pin securely below the drawstring sleeve seam. Fold the fabric down and blind stitch the lining to the squid through the thin fold of fabric below the seam at the bottom of the sleeve. Stitches should be spaced no more than ½" (13mm) apart and should not go all the way through the yarn or be visible anywhere except where the fabric and the yarn touch. Repeat for the other side. Then, unfold the lining and blind stitch the top of the sleeve to the squid, spacing the stitches no more than ¼" (6mm) apart. Again, repeat for the other side.

Then, with the safety pin or bodkin, thread a cord through the sleeves so it forms one complete loop around the opening and then knot the ends together. Repeat with the other cord so the knot is at the opposite opening. Make sure the cords are long enough to easily tie closed when the drawstring is tightened and then trim the ends. To close the bag, pull on the knots and then tie.

To make a 10"–11" (25cm–28cm) thin cord from yarn: Take a 28"–30" (71cm–76cm) piece of DK to worsted-weight yarn. Tie a small loop at both ends, big enough for a finger tip. Securing one end, twist the other end (in the same direction as the twist of the yarn) until the strand is very tightly twisted. Bring the two ends together and allow it to spring into a cord. Smooth the twist along the length if it is uneven, and then knot the two ends together. Trim or untie the previous knots, making sure to leave at least ¼" (6mm) of a tail. Make two.

Hallowed Counsel

Instead of a button, you could also use snaps or hook/loop tape for feeder tentacle strap.

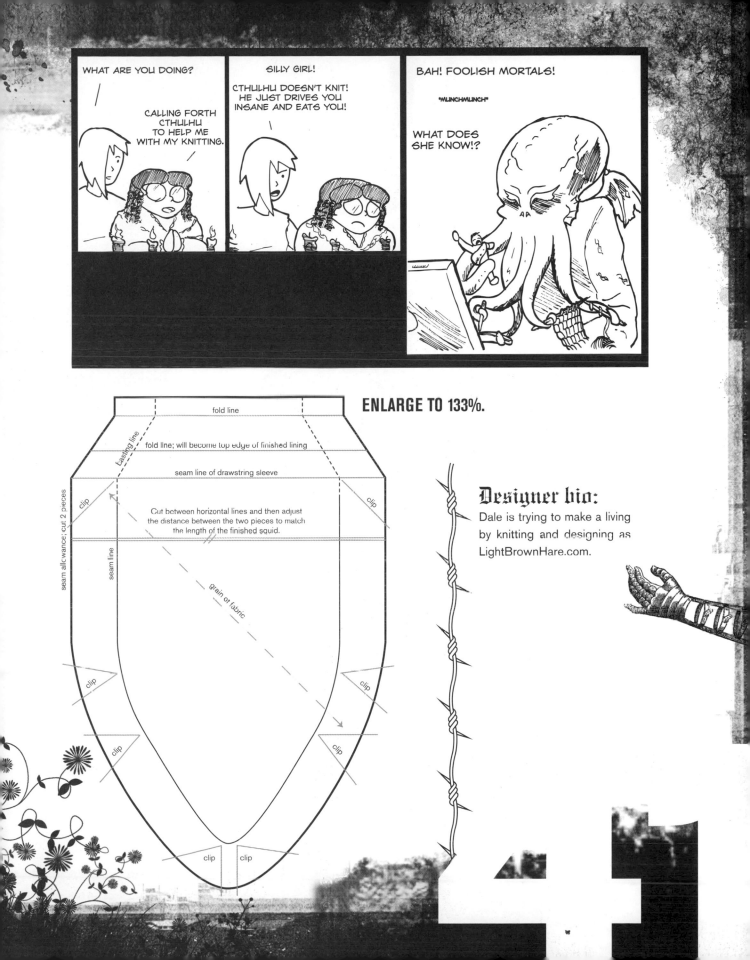

ENLARGE TO 133%.

fold line

basting line

fold line; will become top edge of finished lining

seam line of drawstring sleeve

clip

seam allowance; cut 2 pieces

seam line

Cut between horizontal lines and then adjust the distance between the two pieces to match the length of the finished squid.

grain of fabric

clip

Designer bio:

Dale is trying to make a living by knitting and designing as LightBrownHare.com.

I grew up in a Catholic family and I have always loved the Church's imagery, especially the Virgin Mary. Mary is a strong matriarchal figure and her heart is represented as pure. I collect Catholic paraphernalia so it only seemed natural to add a knitted figure to my collection.

MOOD ENHANCERS:

Any music by Soeur Sourire; episodes of *The Flying Nun*

BY ROBYN WADE

SKILLS USED:

Basic knitting (see page 131)
Knitting in the round (see page 143)
Short rows
Mattress Stitch (see page 142)

MATERIALS AND TOOLS:

1 skein (220 yards or 198 meters) Cascade Yarns 220 100% wool yarn in color 9404 burgundy
1 skein (230 yards or 207 meters) Schoeller & Stahl Fortissima Socka superwash wool/polyamid yarn color 1093 pink
1 skein (230 yards or 207 meters) Schoeller & Stahl Fortissima Socka superwash wool/polyamid yarn color 1003 red (flame MC)
1 skein (230 yards or 207 meters) Schoeller & Stahl Fortissima Socka superwash wool/polyamid yarn color 1008 orange (flame CC1)
1 skein (230 yards or 207 meters) Schoeller & Stahl Fortissima Socka superwash wool/polyamid yarn color 1007 yellow (flame CC2)
1 skein (230 yards or 207 meters) Schoeller & Stahl Fortissima Socka superwash wool/polyamid yarn color 1090 green
1 set US #8 (5mm) double-point needles (or size needed to obtain gauge)
1 set US #1 (2.25mm) double-point needles
1 set US #1 (2.25mm) straight or circular needles (optional)
Stitch markers
Tapestry needle
3 plastic sword-shaped decorative toothpicks
Fiber fill or scrap yarn to stuff the heart
Gold paint (optional)

GAUGE:

16 sts = 4" (10 cm) in stockinette with two strands of Cascade 220 and larger needles
Since this is not meant to be worn, the gauge really isn't important.

FINISHED SIZE:

The finished heart measures 6" (15cm) in height.

NOTES:

The Immaculate Heart is knitted in several pieces and sewn together. The heart is made using two strands of Cascade 220 held together to give it a fuller body. The roses and the leaves are worked flat and can either be made on the US #1 (2.25mm) double-pointed needles used as straight needles or on a set of straight or circular needles.

Heart:

Using larger needles and two strands of Cascade 220 held together, cast on 6 sts. Divide evenly between three needles (2 sts per needle). Join together in a round without twisting the sts.

Round 1: K all sts.

Round 2: Kfb all sts. 12 sts remain.

Round 3: K all sts.

Round 4: K1, Kfb around. 18 sts remain

Round 5: K all sts.

Round 6: K4, M1, Pm, K1, M1, K8, M1, Pm, K1, M1, K4. 22 sts remain.

Rounds 7–8: K all sts.

Round 9: (K to marker, M1, slip marker, K1, M1)×2, K to end. 26 sts remain.

Rounds 10–24: Repeat rounds 7–9. 46 sts remain.

Rounds 25–26: K all sts.

Heart shaping:

Redistribute the sts so the first 23 sts are on one double-point needle and the last 23 sts are on a second double-point needle.

Working only the first 23 stitches, K15, W&t, P8, W&t, *knit to gap, W&t, purl to gap, W&t, rep from * until you W&t around the last stitch, knit to last stitch.

Working only the last 23 stitches, K15, W&t, P8, W&t, *knit to gap, W&t, purl to gap, W&t, rep from * until you W&t around the last stitch, knit to last stitch.

Next round: K2tog to end. 26 sts remain.

Next round: *K1, K2tog, rep from * to last 2 stitches, K2tog. 17 sts remain.

Knit 5 more rnds.

Bind off all sts loosely.

Roses (make eight):

Using smaller needles and pink yarn, cast on 60 sts.

Row 1: K all sts.

Row 2: P all sts.

Row 3: K2tog across all sts. 30 sts remain.

Row 4: P all sts.

Row 5: K2tog across all sts. 15 sts remain.

Row 6: P all sts.

Bind off all sts knit-wise.

With the purl side on the inside, roll into a rose shape and sew a few stitches around the bottom to hold in place.

Leaves (make eight):

The leaves are made in pairs to reduce sewing.

Using smaller needles and green yarn, cast on 3 sts.

Row 1: K all sts.

Row 2 (and all even rows): P all sts.

Row 3: K1, M1, K1, M1, K1.

Row 5: K2, M1, K1, M1, K2.

Row 7: K3, M1, K1, M1, K3.

Row 9: K2, K2tog, K1, Ssk, K2.

Row 11: K1, K2tog, K1, Ssk, K1.

Row 13: K2tog, K1, Ssk.

Repeat Rows 3–13 once more.

Bind off all sts.

Flames (make five):

Using smaller double-point needles and MC, cast on 15 sts. Divide evenly between three needles (5 sts per needle). Join together in a round without twisting the sts.

Rounds 1–10: K MC all sts.

Rounds 11–12: K6 MC, Sl3, K6 MC.

Round 13: (K2 MC, K1 CC1) across all sts.

Rnd 14: (K1 MC, K2 CC1) across all sts.

Rnd 15: K CC1 all sts.

Rnd 16: K6 CC1, K2tog CC1, K7 CC1.

Rnd 17: K CC1 all sts.

Rnd 18: K6 CC1, K2tog CC1, K6 CC1.

Rnd 19: K6 CC1, K2tog CC1, K5 CC1. 12 sts remain.

Rnd 20: (K2 CC1, K1 CC2) across all sts.

Rnd 21: (K1 CC1, K2 CC2) across all sts.

Rnd 22: K CC2 all sts.

Rnd 23: K1 CC2, SSK CC2, K CC2 to last 2 stitches, K2tog CC2.

Rnd 24: K CC2 all sts.

Rnd 25: K1 CC2, SSK CC2, K CC2 to last 2 stitches, K2tog CC2.

Rnd 26: K CC2 all sts.

Rnd 27: K1 CC2, Ssk CC2, K CC2 to last 2 stitches, K2tog CC2. 6 sts remain

Cut the yarn and use the tapestry needle to thread the yarn tail through the remaining sts. Remove the remaining sts from the needles and pull yarn tail to close the end of the flame.

Assembly:

Using the fiber fill or yarn scraps, stuff the heart. Loosely stuff the flames and sew them together in a cluster. Sew the top of the heart shut with the flames coming out the aorta. Bend each set of leaves into a 45-degree angle and sew the leaves in a band around the body of the heart. Sew the roses on top of the leaves. Finally, paint the three plastic swords gold and stick them into the upper right section of the heart in a cluster.

Designer bio:

Robyn Wade has always been into fiber arts–from sewing to crochet to knitting. While she likes knitted clothing, she really loves to spend time knitting less practical items like body parts and inanimate objects. Robyn currently lives in Lexington, Kentucky, where she co-owns a knit and craft shop called ReBelle (www.ReBellegirls.com).

45

YAR!

BY MICHELLE BOOHER

We ... are men without a country. Outlaws in our own land and homeless outcasts in any other. Desperate men, we go to seek a desperate fortune. Therefore, we do here and now band ourselves into a brotherhood of buccaneers . . . to practice the trade of piracy on the high seas. We, the hunted, will now hunt! —Captain Blood, 1935

Ahoy, me hearties! This double knit, reversible cap is packed fore to aft with so much pirattitude that it walks the thin line between campy and totally awesome. Everyone has a little bit of a pirate in them, whether they be a pirate of the high seas, of the high frequencies, or of the high bandwidth usage (you know who you are), so why not fly your colors with pride? Best of all, the hats are really cheap to make, so when your hearties start demanding Yar! hats of their own, it won't cost you a fistful of pieces of eight to oblige.

MOOD ENHANCERS:

Captain Blood (1935); *The Sea Hawk* (1940); *The Rime of the Ancient Mariner* by Samuel Taylor Coleridge

SKILLS USED:

Basic knitting (see page 131)
Knitting in the round (see page 143)

MATERIALS AND TOOLS:

1 skein (110 yards or 99 meters) Knit Picks Wool of the Andes 100% wool yarn in color Coal (MC)
1 skein (110 yards or 99 meters) Knit Picks Wool of the Andes 100% wool yarn in color Cranberry (CC)
1 set US #5 (3.75mm) double-point needles (or size needed to obtain gauge)
1 US #5 (3.75mm) 16" (41cm) circular needle (or size needed to obtain gauge)
Stitch markers
Tapestry needle
Waste yarn or stitch holders

GAUGE:

24 sts × 32 rows = 4" (10cm) in stockinette stitch

FINISHED SIZE:

Circumference: 19" (48cm)

NOTES:

The reversible nature of this hat and the extra warmth are achieved through a process known as double knitting. If you've ever worked up an especially firm 1 × 1 rib and noticed how it pulled together until it seemed to show stockinette stitch on both sides of the fabric, then you'll have a good idea of how double knitting works.

In two-color double knitting, each square on the chart represents two stitches: the stitch that will show on the "right side" (the side facing you as you work the hat), which is knitted, and the stitch that will show on the "wrong side," which is purled. This can be hard to keep track of at first, but once you find your rhythm, it becomes much easier. When working the stitches, it helps to keep an even tension, reasonably firm but not too tight.

SPECIAL STITCHES:

Double Knit (DK)

With both yarns to the back, K1 with MC. Bring MC and CC yarn to the front of the work. With CC, P1. Bring both yarns to the back of the work. Repeat.

When you come to a square on the chart where the CC should show on the side facing you, purl the MC stitch that corresponds to that square and knit the CC stitch.

Double Knit Decrease

Change the order of the next 4 sts from MC, CC, MC, CC to MC, MC, CC, CC. While maintaining a firm tension, K2tog MC, Ssp CC. The goal of the double knit decrease is to execute a K2tog decrease while preserving the look of the double knit fabric.

Hat:

With circular needle, cast on 150 sts in MC. Join together in a round without twisting the sts. Place marker at the beginning of the round.

Work all rounds of the skull and crossbones chart. When working the first round of the chart, place a marker after each repeat of the chart. On subsequent rounds, the chart will be repeated after each marker.

When the chart indicates a decrease, work the chart to the last four stitches before each marker and then work a double knit decrease. Change to double-point needles when the hat's circumference becomes too small for a circular needle. When all rows of the chart have been completed, 60 sts remain.

Finishing:

Separate the MC and CC stitches, placing the MC stitches on waste yarn or stitch holders. Cut the CC yarn, leaving a 16" (41cm) tail. Thread the CC yarn through all of the CC stitches while removing them from the needles. Pull the yarn tight, and secure. Repeat with MC stitches. Weave in ends.

Designer bio:

I've always loved to design clothing. My father still jokes about how when I was little, the first thing I'd do with a new doll was rip off all of its clothes so I could tape on new ones made lovingly out of tissue paper and decorated with stickers and glitter. I'm still that little girl at heart, stickers, glitter . . . I generally don't rip off people's clothes, however, unless they want me to.

My job as manager at In Sheep's Clothing, my local yarn shop, provides me with ample exposure to beautiful yarn and creative people and serves as a constant source of inspiration. When I'm not knitting, I can be found hanging out at Café Roma, tinkering with my eternally unfinished novel (next year, Dad, I promise!), making a fool of myself at live-action role-playing games, and curling up at home to watch old movies with my fiancée, Sam, and my two kitties, Cordelia and don Francisco.

Hallowed Counsel

When using interchangeable needles in the round, you'll knit faster if you put a smaller needle on the left side.

—Robyn Wade

History of the Skull and Crossbones

According to the "Internets," the familiar skull-and-crossbones symbol is actually connected to the Knights Templar—those old European dudes who felt the need to fight holy war after holy war in the name of Christianity. Mind you, the Internet also has a bazillion versions of these histories, so here we've pieced them together into a coherent whole for you. Some (or more likely all) of what follows might be entirely false, and for once, it won't be false just because we decided to make it up!

The Knights carried a red flag and at some point a band of them went nautical, fighting against the Pope. They believed that only one's skull and two bones needed to be buried properly to ensure entrance to Heaven. The hill where Christ was crucified was referred to as Golgotha, "the place of the skull," hence the burying of the skull, and the cross was then symbolized as two crossed bones. The Knights were said to mark their fallen comrades' graves this way. Once disbanded by the Church, the remaining sailing Knights became the seed of piracy that blossomed in the Late Middle Ages. Early pirates flew red and black flags, raising one to communicate their intentions. A black flag meant they would take prisoners for ransom, and was often flown first to give the victims a chance to surrender. The red flag (in French, *jolie rouge*) meant they would take no prisoners—they meant to kill everyone, rather like the Crusaders did in an effort to cleanse the world of the unworthy heathens. (Genocide much?) The old skull and crossbones was added to the black flag to imply that the pirates really meant business, and many pirates did variations on this theme with cutlasses and hourglasses, etc., so that you could tell exactly which pirate was about to pillage, plunder, and generally make not-nice with your booty. The *jolie rouge* was then bastardized—er, we mean Anglicized—into the Jolly Roger, even though the Jolly Roger has a black background and not a red one.

And then an evil fairy put a curse on all pirates to wear shiny pants and sing and dance, which lead to their eventual demise. In the meanwhile, the skull-and-crossbones was usurped by the 1970s British punk movement. Sid Vicious then licensed the image to Hot Topic stores for one hundred years, or until Bollywood actress Aishwarya Bachchan (née Rai) wins an Oscar for her breakthrough performance as a developmentally disabled maidservant who rises to politcal power and ushers in a new era of equality for lower caste Indians, whichever happens first.[1]

[1]OK, we couldn't resist lying a little! (again)

Source: Teh Internets

CHET

Crocheters are not called hookers because they work with hooks, but rather because the first crocheter was Captain Hook. He first used a small hook on a stick to make loops with string, but later—*tick tock, tick tock*—lost his hand to a crocodile. Rather than choosing a state-of-the-art replacement hand, he went with a hook so he could continue the passion for what he had dubbed "Crotchety." (This was later mistakenly changed to "crochet" by some snooty dead white men who thought Captain Hook was French.) He named it Crotchety to indicate his state of mind while trying to get the correct number of wraps on the hook for a half double crochet. No longer able to rub his hands together for warmth without causing himself serious injury, he created the granny square, which he named after his uncle, Col. Granny Smith, who also had lost a hand in a tragic reptile-related accident during the Second World War. Captain Hook would later be more widely known as a fearsome pirate, but deep down, all hookers know better.

51

BRIER ROSE

BY JENNIFER FLETCHER

No need (nor desire) for a prince to save you from this thorny brier. Two roses in full bloom adorn this vine-like crocheted scarflette, complete with two styles of leaves.

MOOD ENHANCERS:

Snow White, Blood Red edited by Ellen Datlow and Terri Windling

SKILLS USED:

Basic crochet (see page 145)
Picot (as explained in project instructions)

MATERIALS AND TOOLS:

1 skein (68 yards or 61 meters) Knit Picks Panache alpaca/cashmere/silk/merino yarn in color Moss (A)
1 skein (68 yards or 61 meters) Knit Picks Panache alpaca/cashmere/silk/merino yarn in color Cranberry (C)
1 skein (68 yards or 61 meters) Knit Picks Panache alpaca/cashmere/silk/merino yarn in color Mulled Wine (D)
1 skein (121 yards or 109 meters) Knit Picks Decadence alpaca yarn in color Spring Leaf (B)
1 US H/8 (5mm) crochet hook
1 US J/10 (6mm) crochet hook
Tapestry needle
Open loop stitch markers (optional)
Press cloth (optional)

GAUGE:

16 sts x 8 rows = 4" (10cm) in dc with H hook and yarn A

FINISHED SIZE:

63" (160cm) long (excluding leaves)

SPECIAL STITCHES:

Small thorn (sc-picot st)

Sc in st, ch 3, sl st in 3rd ch from hook, then sl st by inserting hook in between the horizontal loops of sc, and through the side of that sc, yo, and pull up a loop.

Large thorn (dc-picot st)

Dc in st, ch 4, sl st in 3rd ch from hook, sl st in next ch, sl st by inserting hook in between the horizontal loops of the dc, and through the side of that dc (top section of dc only), yo, and pull up a loop.

When making stitches on top of rounds with picots, make a stitch behind the picot, either in the back loop (for sc-picot) or into a loop behind at the base picot (for dc-picot).

NOTES:

Make stitches in both horizontal loops of stitches unless otherwise noted. Do not join rounds unless otherwise noted. Numbers in [ ] indicate the number of stitches in that row.

The following directions make reference to the adjustable ring. If you are not familiar with with this method, there are several tutorials available online. It is simply an easier way of crocheting in the round.

Thorny Vine:

With Color A and H/8 hook:

Round 1: 4 sc into adj ring. [4]

Rounds 2–4: Sc in ea st around. [4]

Round 5: 2 sc in next st, sc in ea rem st around [5]

Round 6: Sc in ea st around. [5]

Round 7: Sc-picot st in front loop only of next st, sc in ea rem st around. [5]

Round 8: Sc next st, 2 sc in next st, sc in ea rem st around. [6]

Round 9: Sc in ea st around. [6]

Rounds 10–11: 2 sc in next st, sc in ea rem st around. [8]

Rounds 12–14: Sc in ea st around. [8]

Round 15: Sc-picot st in front loop only of next st, sc in ea rem st around. [8]

Round 16: 2 hdc in next st, hdc in ea rem st around. [9]

Rounds 17–18: Hdc in ea st around. [9]

Rounds 19–21: Dc in ea st around. [9]

Round 22: Dc-picot st in next st, dc in ea rem st around. [9]

Round 23: 2 dc in next st, dc in ea rem st around. [10]

Rounds 24–25: Dc in ea st around. [10]

Round 26: 2 dc in next st, dc in ea rem st around. [11]

Round 27: Dc in ea st around. [11]

Round 28: Dc in next 4 st, dc-picot st in next st, dc in ea rem st around. [11]

Continue adding to the length of the vine, working in dc and adding dc-picot sts every 2"–4" (5cm-10cm). Stagger the thorns around the vine. Work until the vine measures 56" (142cm), or desired length. End with a row containing a dc-picot st.

Decrease Round 1: Work 1 dec-dc over next 2 st, dc in ea rem st around. [10]

Decrease Round 2: Dc in ea st around. [10]

Decrease Round 3: Work 1 dec-dc over next 2 st, dc in ea rem st around. [9]

Decrease Round 4: Hdc in ea st around. [9]

Decrease Round 5: Sc in ea st around. [9]

Decrease Rounds 7–8: Work 1 dec-sc in next 2 st, sc in ea rem st around. [7]

Decrease Round 9: Sc in ea st around. [7]

Decrease Round 10: Work 1 dec-sc in next 2 sts, sc in ea rem st around. [6]

Decrease Round 11: Sc in ea st around. [6]

Decrease Round 12: (Work 1 dec-sc in next 2 st)×3. [3]

Leaf at Tip:

Foundation chain: Ch 10, break yarn and loosely attach Color B, ch 1.

Round 1: Sl st in 2nd ch from hook, sl st in next 2 ch, sc in next ch, dc in next ch, tr in next ch, dc in next ch, sc in next ch, ch 2. Working around foundation chain to the opposite side, sc in same ch as previous sc, dc in next ch, tr in next ch, dc in next ch, sc in next ch, sl st in ea rem 2 ch, fasten off.

Small Leaf (make 3 bi-color leaves, 4 solid leaves):

With Color A and H/8 hook, begin with a 6" (15cm) tail to secure the leaf to the vine.

Foundation chain: Ch 12. For solid leaves, begin Round 1. For bi-color leaves, break yarn, loosely attach Color B, ch 1.

Round 1: Sl st in 2nd ch from hook, sl st in next ch, sc in next ch, dc in next ch, tr in next ch, dc in next ch, sc in next ch, ch 2. Working around foundation chain to the opposite side, sc in same ch as previous sc, dc in next ch, tr in next ch, dc in next ch, sc in next ch, sl st in ea rem 3 ch, fasten off.

Pointed Leaf (make 4 bi-color leaves, 4 solid leaves):

With Color A and H/8 hook, begin with a 6" (15cm) tail to secure the leaf to vine.

Foundation chain: Ch 12. For solid leaves, begin Round 1. For bi-color leaves, break yarn, loosely attach Color B, ch 1.

Round 1: Sl st in 2nd ch from hook, sl st in next ch, sc in next 2 ch, dc in next ch, tr in next ch, dc in next ch, sc in next ch, ch 2. Working around foundation chain to the opposite side, sc in same ch as previous sc, dc in next ch, tr in next ch, dc in next ch, sc in next ch, sl st in ea rem 3 ch, fasten off.

3-Leaf Cluster (make one):

Cut three 28" (71cm) pieces of yarn (A). With J/10 hook, leave a 6" (15cm) tail to secure the leaves to the vine and ch 3 with all three strands of yarn held together. Change to H/8 hook and work with the middle strand of yarn.

Leaf 1: Ch 12, follow directions for bi-color Small Leaf.

Leaves 2 and 3: Insert hook into the base of the 3 strands, yo and pull up a loop of 1 of the rem strands. Follow directions for bi-color Small Leaf, but ch 9 instead of ch 12. Repeat for Leaf 3.

Roses (make two):

With Color C and H/8 hook:

Center

Round 1: 5 sc into adj ring, join, ch 1. [5]

Round 2: Sc in ea st around, join, ch 1. [5]

Round 3: 2 sc in ea st around, join, ch 1. [10]

Inside Petals

Round 4: Working in front loops only *(sc, ch 1, dc, ch 1, sc) in next st, sl st in next st; rep from * around, break yarn. (5 petals)

With Color D and H/8 hook, attach new color, ch 1.

Round 5: Working in back loops only *sc in next st, 2 sc in next st; rep from * around, join, ch 1. [15]

Middle and Outside Petals

Round 6: Working in front loops only *(sc, hdc, dc) in next st, (dc, hdc, sc) in next st, sl st in next st; rep from * around, ch 1. (5 petals)

Round 7: Working in back loops only, *Sl st in next st, (hdc, dc, tr) in next st, (tr, dc, hdc) in next st; rep from * around, fasten off. (5 petals)

Finishing:

Weave in ends, except for the tails at the end of the leaf stems. Distribute the leaves as desired along the vine. With a tapestry needle, use leaf tails to attach the leaves to the vine. With color A, sew on roses 18" (46cm) apart approximately in the middle of the vine, or where desired. Lightly press backside of leaves with a press cloth.

Designer bio:

Jennifer learned to crochet in college as a way to deal with stress and avoid homework. She's been hooked (pun intended) ever since, concocting imaginative and wearable accessories inspired by fairytales, flora, and fauna. Through her company, Fable Handmade Goods, Jennifer shares her love for crochet with other crafters. The website, www.fablehandmadegoods .com, offers free stuff and downloadable patterns for sale.

LIZA'S NET

BY KATHRYN MILLER

I's the b'y that builds the boat
And I's the b'y that sails her
I's the b'y that catches the fish
And takes them home to Lizer
—*Traditional Newfoundland folk song*

Fish nets have been requisite equipment for the economic welfare of many coastal areas for generations; necessary for catching and hauling in sustenance for one community or a country. In part they symbolize a long heritage of hard work, struggle and often lonely times for fisher-folk. While they have a practical function, "fish nets" also elicit a juxtaposed image of a sexy, delicate garment fabric that both exposes and covers the flesh. I wanted to create a garment in crochet that demonstrates the latter.

These gloves are named after the fisherman's wife in the Newfoundland folk song "I's the B'y." In my mind, Liza evokes a kind of paradox as well. I imagine her as a lonely woman with her b'y out at sea, living in a cold and isolated, yet beautiful, place in the late 1800s. She would know first-hand this heritage of hard times and uncertainty. If Liza wanted something pretty for herself, it would have to be handmade by her out of affordable materials; she would crochet. The practical function of these gloves is not so much that they work to protect the hand as many gloves do, but is rather in their delicacy, the baring and enclosing of toiling hands.

MOOD ENHANCERS:

"I'se the B'ye" *Great Big Sea* by Great Big Sea

SKILLS USED:

Basic crochet (see page 145)

MATERIALS AND TOOLS:

1 ball (350 yards or 315 meters) J&P Coats Royale Classic Crochet 100% mercerized cotton thread in color 0012 Black
US #3 (2.1mm) steel crochet hook
Size 10 crochet thread
Sewing needle
Two small buttons in a matching or contrasting color

GAUGE:

10 (ch 4, dc) spaces plus turning chain space
× 16 rows = 4" (10cm)
This stitch pattern will stretch, so it is important to shape the gauge swatch, but to avoid stretching it taut when measuring. The spaces should be even.

FINISHED SIZE:

Sizes: Women's S–M (L–XL)
7 (8)" [18 (20) cm] circumference around the knuckles

Begin gloves:

Foundation Row: Ch 70 (78).
Row 1: Turn. Ch 8, sk 1 ch of foundation row *dc in next ch, ch 4, sk 3 ch of foundation row. Repeat * across, end with dc. [17 (19) sp.]
Row 2: Turn. Ch 8, *dc in next ch 4 sp, ch 4. Repeat from * across, end with dc in turning ch sp.
Repeat Row 2 until work measures 4 (5)" 10 (13)cm, or 16 (20) rows, or desired palm length. Do not fasten off.

Left hand finger shaping:

Join the end of the final palm row to the turning ch at the beginning of the row with a sl st, forming a tube shape with the fabric. Keep the open edge of the tube even to accommodate the thumb. The fabric will cover the back side of the hand, then wrap around the pinky side of the hand, and will cover the palm side.

To shape the left hand, begin by working the back side, RS facing, and cross over to the palm side, WS facing: This will connect the back and palm sides of the glove between each finger. Because the fabric is now a tube, for the left hand, the back RS facing and palm WS facing both face in the same way.

For S–M:

*(Ch 4, dc) in next 2 ch 4 sp on back side RS facing, (ch 4, dc in ch 4 sp) on palm side WS facing directly behind next st. Repeat from * twice more. Do not sk sts on backside; only sk sts on palm side. Do not break off but continue to shape pinky finger.

For L–XL:

*(Ch 4, dc) in next 2 ch 4 sp on back side RS facing, (ch 4, dc in ch 4 sp) on palm side WS facing directly behind next st, sk next back side sp. Repeat from * twice more. Do not break off but continue to shape pinky finger.

Right hand finger shaping:

For S–M:

*(Ch 4, dc) in next 2 ch 4 sp on palm side RS facing, (ch 4, dc in ch 4 sp) on back side WS facing directly behind next st. Repeat from * twice more. Do not sk sts on palm side; only sk sts on back side. Do not break off but continue to shape pinky finger.

For L–XL:

*(Ch 4, dc) in next 2 ch 4 sp on palm side RS facing, (ch 4, dc in ch 4 sp) on back side WS facing directly behind next st, sk next palm side sp. Repeat from * twice more. Do not break off but continue to shape pinky finger.

Pinky finger:

(Ch 4, dc) in next 2 st. (ch 4, dc) around to next palm side sp. Work (ch 4, dc) around until next worked space; sk previously worked sp. (Ch 4, dc) evenly in a spiral around in each sp until desired length, ending between the fingers. Sc around in each space to close opening and fasten off. Weave in end to close the opening.

Ring, middle and index fingers:

Join with sl st between fingers. (Ch 6, dc) in next sp. Work (ch 4, dc) evenly in a spiral around in each sp until desired length, ending between the fingers. Sc around in each space to close opening and fasten off. Weave in ends to close the openings. Repeat for each finger.

Open edge:

Join thread at base of index finger and evenly sl st the back and palm sides together, until approximately half-way down the open edge, or until the edge meets the thumb. Fasten off.

Gusset and thumb:

Join with sl st in bottom edge corner and sl st together the open edge for one inch. (Ch 6, dc) in next edge sp. *(Ch 4, dc) around until sp before open edge seam and (ch 4, dc) around. Repeat * once. (Ch 4, dc) around as in other fingers until desired length. Fasten off.

Cuff:

The cuff is worked with the bottom edge upward-facing.

Foundation row: Join thread with sl st in the bottom edge, at the outside (pinky side) of the hand. Ch 8, dc in next sp. *Ch 4, dc in next ch 4 sp. Repeat from * across the bottom edge, ending with dc in the same sp as beginning ch 8. Do not join.

Row 1: Turn. Ch 8, dc in next sp. *Ch 4, dc in next ch 4 sp. Repeat from * across to end of row.

Repeat Row 1 until cuff is desired length, ending with a WS row.

Next Row: Turn. Ch 1. *(3 sc, ch 3, 3 sc) in next ch 4 sp. Repeat from * across to end of the row.

Next Row: Sc around the cuff row edges. Fasten off.

Finishing:

Attach button. Join thread opposite button with sl st and ch short chain for button loop.

Designer bio:

Kathryn Miller lives in Toronto, Ontario, Canada, with her husband and cat. She is an avid crocheter from a long line of needleworkers and can be found at www.dainty-kate.livejournal.com.

Tap into the Dark Side

Get ready for a night of candlelit introspection:

1. Put on our favorite song from The Smiths, "Asleep." Set your player to infinite repeat.
2. Turn off all the lights in the house.
3. Stumble blindly around looking for matches and candles.
4. Turn the lights back on.
5. Arrange and light candles.
6. Don't forget to turn the lights back off!
7. Welcome in the darkness. If you aren't suitably depressed by the fifth repeat of the song, you may want to consider joining another crafting subculture.

WHY THE ANTICRAFT LOVES...

Christopher Moore
Zombies, vampires, stupid angels, the Grim Reaper, and the gospel according to Biff. Squeegasmic!

Deepak Chopra
The Seven Spiritual Laws of Success got us where we are today. Or it might have, if we had read it.

Dick Clark
We feel strongly about supporting the Lich community.

Heather Graham
Best pretend porn star ever.

H.P. Lovecraft
Do we even need to say why? Cthulu, Cthulu, Cthulu!

John Denver
"It makes me giggle."

Martha Stewart
Come on. You don't get that famous for crafting without invoking dark forces.

Sark
She's got more markers than the entire population of Europe and she's not afraid to let her freak flag fly.

LILY

BY TONKS

This pattern is based on a traditional Victorian lace edging. It all started when I wanted to recreate something akin to the necklace Lily finds at the vanity in the movie *Legend*.

MOOD ENHANCERS:

Legend (1985, rated PG)

SKILLS USED:

Basic crochet (see page 145)
Basic sewing

MATERIALS AND TOOLS:

Crochet cotton and a steel crochet hook. (You know, the tiny tiny ones.) The size of the hook is up to you—the larger the steel hook, the more volume the choker has.
Small tapestry needle
Sewing needle or beading needle
Sewing or beading thread to match choker,
or invisible thread
Assortment of beads to suit your taste (if you want seed beads, use the beading needle!)
Length of ribbon at least a foot long, or necklace fastener of your choice
Pretty brooch (optional)

Choker:

Foundation Row: Ch 12.
Row 1: Turn. Dc in 6th ch from hook, ch 2, dc in same stitch, ch 2, skip 2 chs, sc in next ch, ch 2, skip 2 chs, (dc, ch 2, dc) in next ch, ch 3.
Row 2: Turn. (Dc, ch 2, dc) in 1st ch 2 space, ch 3, skip next ch 2 spaces, 5 dc in next ch 2 space, ch 5.
Row 3: Turn. (Dc, ch 2, dc) in 3rd dc, ch 2, sc in ch 3 loop, ch 2, (dc, ch 2, dc) in next ch 2 space, ch 3.
Repeat Rows 2 and 3 until work measures approximately 1½" (4cm) less than the circumference of your neck. End with Row 2.

Turn the work and work down the ch 5 side of the piece as follows:
Row 1: *Ch 2, [(dc, ch 1)×6, dc] in first ch 5 space, ch 2, sc in next ch 5 space * to end of choker and turn.
Row 2: *Ch 3, dc in 1st ch 1 space, (ch 5, dc in next ch 1 space)×5, ch 3, sc in sc, rep from * to end. Fasten off.

Ornamentation:

Now for the fun part! Use the beads to decorate the choker in any way you see fit. If you are using a centerpiece for the choker, find the center of the choker base by folding it end to end. Mark the spot with extra yarn and avoid putting beads in that particular spot, as it will disrupt how the brooch lies. Using the beading method of your choice, put your beads in whatever spaces you fancy. This could be a very simple piece, or a heavily beaded work of art. 'Sup to you. When you're done beading, secure the thread and weave in all the ends using the small tapestry needle. Attach the ribbon by simply threading it through the ends or attach the closure of your choice to officially make it a choker. Place your broach, if you're using one, in the center of your choker and admire your work.

Variations:

Use extra beads to create draping from the choker. When doing this, let the piece drape over your knee or a secure rounded object similar to your neck to make sure the draping lays correctly.

Brooches are my favorite, but you can use just about anything as a centerpiece. I also recommend old chandelier crystals, interesting charms, unique appliqué, or anything else that catches your fancy. I've even used skull zipper pulls.

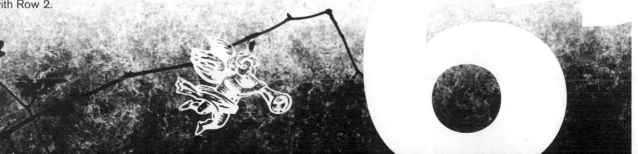

Designer bio:

Tonks, so named for her naturally bubblegum-pink hair, has a serious yarn fetish and will covet any and all fibers possible for the simple joy of having them in her home. Growing up in Wisconsin with her equally fabulous mother taught Tonks to appreciate knitwear at a very young age, although she loathes making hats. Tonks turned her abundant love of yarn into a home-based business catering to the underground scene. She now lives outside of Washington DC, with her fiber-bearing pets and a very patient, tolerant husband. You can find Tonks playing with yarn and other toys of delight at www.weavingroses.com.

A Bucketful of Hummus

*

⅔ *lb. dry chickpeas (garbanzo beans)*
6 cups filtered water
2 tablespoons salt
OR replace dry chickpeas, filtered water, and salt
with 4 cups of drained, canned chickpeas.
¼ *cup fresh lemon juice*
4 cloves garlic, peeled
3 whole scallions (green onions)
2 heaping spoonfuls plain yogurt
6 tablespoons tahini
2 shallot cloves, peeled
2 tablespoons extra virgin olive oil
¼ *teaspoon ground cumin*
¼ *teaspoon cayenne pepper (ground red pepper)*

In a large bowl, soak chickpeas overnight in cold water. The bowl should be large enough to cover the chickpeas with 1–2" (3–4cm) of water. The next day, discard soaking water. Simmer chickpeas, covered, with 6 cups of filtered water and 2 table-spoons of salt for 4–6 hours until completely tender. You can also cook them in a Crock Pot on low heat for 6–8 hours. This takes much longer than using canned chickpeas, but will taste much better. Drain chickpeas. You can reserve the liquid to use as stock in other recipes—it has a wonderful silky texture. To save the stock, bring the temperature down quickly and freeze what you will not use within the next day.

Wash scallions and remove roots—remove excess green leaves if desired. In a food processor, mix drained chickpeas with all other ingredients and process to your desired texture. This is a more Greek-style hummus; for a more Middle Eastern style, add more tahini but less garlic and no scallions, and process until very smooth. Extra hummus also freezes very well in an airtight container with a piece of waxed paper or plastic wrap over the top to reduce exposed surfaces. Let thaw overnight in the refrigerator and stir well before serving.

Makes approx. 4½ cups hummus.

Bloodcicle (Frozen Sangria)

1 large can frozen orange juice concentrate, partially thawed
1 box frozen strawberries (thawed)
1 large bottle of your favorite red wine
Sugar to taste
Fresh fruit for garnish

Crush strawberries. In a large plastic pitcher or punch-bowl, add strawberries, frozen orange juice, and 2 canfuls of water. Mix well and taste. Sweeten with sugar if desired. Add red wine. Place in freezer and stir once an hour until fully frozen. Serve in a tall glass with a long-handled spoon and fruit garnish.

DUNGEON DÉCOR

BY MEGAN GRANHOLM AND TONKS

THE CAPTAIN'S DAUGHTER

Megan Granholm

The old song "What Do You Do with a Drunken Sailor" sometimes includes the verse "give him a taste of the Captain's Daughter," which is not as sexy as it might sound. The Captain's Daughter was a nickname for the cat o' nine tails. Back in the days of pirates and drunken sailors, captains punished the wrongdoings of their men by lashing their backs with a whip made of rope or animal hide. This whip had nine braided thongs, sometimes knotted a few times down the length of the braids to encourage more pain to the victim. These days, however, a taste of the Captain's Daughter can be quite sexy (assuming everyone is a consenting adult). It only takes one or two evenings to crochet your own cat o' nine tails, and then you can teach your favorite pirate a lesson.

MOOD ENHANCERS:

Exit to Eden (1994, rated R) if you're looking for laughs;
Exit to Eden by Anne Rice, otherwise

SKILLS USED:

Basic crochet (see page 145)
Front post double crochet (see page 151)
Back post double crochet (see page 151)

MATERIALS AND TOOLS:

1 spool (109 yards or 98 meters) 1mm waxed cotton cording, or 1mm leather cord
approximately 50 yards (46m) worsted weight yarn the same color or a shade darker than your cording, or in a sharply contrasting color if you're feeling cheeky
US G/6 (4mm) crochet hook
US I/9 (5.5mm) crochet hook
⅝" (16mm) wooden dowel, cut to 5½" (14cm)
Tapestry needle
Large-eyed darning needle

Handle padding

With yarn and G/6 hook:
Foundation Round: Ch 2, 8 sc in 2nd ch.
Round 1: Sc in blo of each st.
Round 2: Sc in flo of each st.
Repeat Round 2 until work measures 2" (5cm). Stretch work around the end of the dowel.
Next Round: So tightly in flo of each st.
Repeat until work reaches ½" (13mm) from the end of the dowel.
Next Round: Ch 2. *Fpdc around first st, bpdc around next st. Repeat from * across. End with sl st in the top of the ch 2. Fasten off, leaving a long tail. Weave the tail through the fpdc and bpdc stitches and pull tight around the dowel.

Thongs (tails!):

With cotton or leather and I/9 hook, start with a 4" (10cm) tail, ch 50. Fasten off, leaving a 4" (10cm) tail. Repeat 8 times.

Thread a large-eyed darning needle with one of the tails. Insert the needle into the center of the end of the dowel, and run the cord under the yarn and down the dowel. Cut off any excess cord. Repeat for each thong.

Handle, part 2:

With cotton or leather and G/6 hook:
Foundation Round: Ch 2, 9 sc in 2nd ch.
Round 1: Sc in blo of each st around.
Round 2: Sc in flo of each st around.

Repeat Round 2 until work measures 1" (2.5cm). Stretch work around end of dowel. This step is a bit difficult because the yarn tends to slip and stretch, making it hard for the cording to stay on the end. The easiest way to complete this step is to turn the tube inside-out, place it over the end of the dowel, and flip the edges down over the dowel. It may be a good idea to hold the dowel between your knees and keep a thumb on the cording while you make a few tight stitches, so the cording dooon't slip off.
Next Round: Sc tightly in flo of each st.

Repeat until work reaches ½" (13mm) from the end of the dowel. Pause every few stitches at first to pull the cording down the dowel with your crochet hook or thumbnails so the tube is snug at the butt of the dowel.
Next Round: Ch 2, *fpdc around first st, bpdc around next st. Repeat from * across.
Fasten off, leaving a long tail. Weave the tail through the fpdc and bpdc stitches and pull tight around the nine tails.

Wrist strap

Cut a piece of cord long enough to fit around your hand, plus a few inches (or centemeters). Thread the darning needle with the cord and thread it through the stitches at the butt end of the whip. Knot the ends together. Alternately, you may wish to use yarn in place of cord for the wrist strap so it's easier on your wrist.

65

KINKS

Tonks

While knitters get to play with pointy sticks, we crocheters are a kinky bunch, too! Kinks was designed with the idea that not all bondage cuffs have to be pink and fluffy to be comfortable. These babies are made with crochet nylon, making them breathable, bearable, and totally wearable—kinky, yet cozy. Tested and approved, my darlings!

MOOD ENHANCERS:

Secretary (2002, rated R)

SKILLS USED:

Basic crochet (see page 145)

MATERIALS AND TOOLS:

1 ball (150 yards) nylon crochet thread, size 5
1" (2.5cm) D rings, 2
US G/6 (4mm) crochet hook
Cigarette lighter or matches

GAUGE:

20 sc × 16 rows = 4" (10cm)

FINISHED SIZE:

2½" × 10½" (6cm ×27cm)

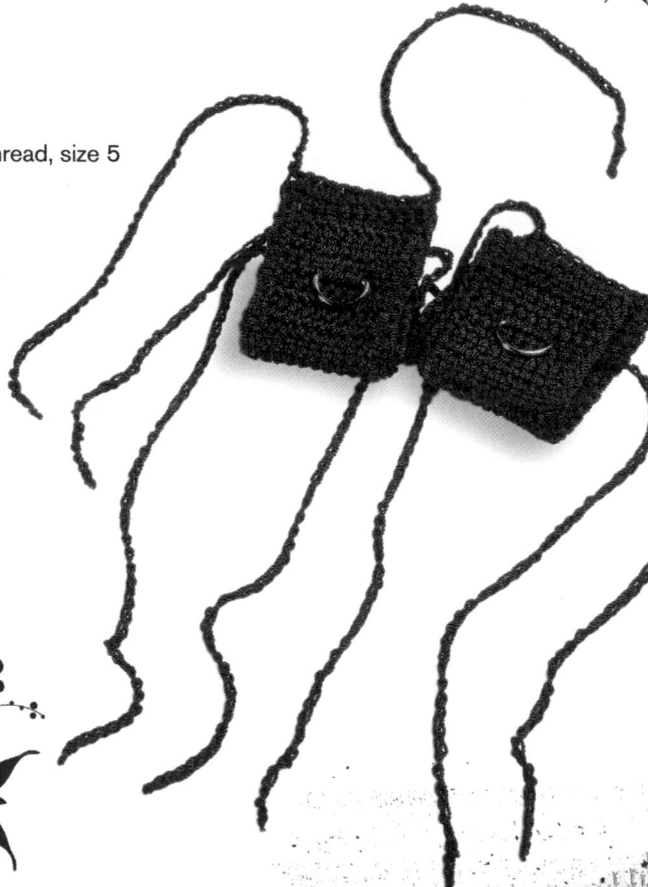

66

Foundation Row: Ch 11.

Row 1: Sc in 2nd ch and each ch across. Ch 1, turn. [10]

Row 2: Sc in each st across. Ch 1, turn. [10]

Repeat Row 2 until work measures 5″ (13cm).

Next Row: Sc in next 3 sc, sc through D ring in next 4 sc, sc in 3 sc. Ch 1, turn.

Repeat Row 2 until work measures 10" (25cm). The D ring will lie in the center of the piece all around. Work a sc edge around the entire piece.

For ties, at each corner, join thread with sl st and ch 45. Use a lighter to melt the yarn ends so they don't unravel.

To wear, put on wrist and wrap ends around and through the D ring. Continue wrapping the ties around until they are back at the underside of your wrist and tie them together. Clip the D ring to whatever support or restraint you wish, or simply clip the D rings together behind your back, you naughty, naughty crafter. And should they be in need of cleaning, you can simply machine wash gentle and dry flat.

Designer bios:

Megan

I am happy to say that I remember something I learned in college! In my freshman year I lived in the dorms, and made friends with the girl down the hall. We'd sit on her bed in the evenings and chat, and I would stare at her hands as she crocheted huge granny square afghans. I finally asked her to teach me, and I spent that night ignoring my tension problems and making a huge granny square as well. Since that was the extent of my neighbor's expertise, I struck out on my own after that, starting with baby steps (an afghan of several small granny squares rather than just one big one!) and then teaching myself how to read and eventually write my own patterns. I tend to leave the dirty dishes in the sink so I can crochet just a little longer. You can visit me (no, not physically, that's kind of creepy) at www.loopdedoo. blogspot.com.

Tonks

To read about Tonks, see page 62.

APOTHECARY TOTE / I [SKULL] TROUBLE TOTE

You can fit all your thumbscrews, skeleton keys, and bone saws in this generously sized crochet tote. Both the solid-colored Apothecary Tote and the striped I [skull] Trouble Tote are lined to add strength and durability. The tote body is made using a seamless crochet technique, so there are no seams to worry about. You can add embroidery or cross stitch to the finished totes by stitching through the evenly spaced holes of the single crochet. If neither design radiates an appropriately vulgar "kiss off!" message to the world for your tastes, I've included a complete alphabet so you can say anything you damn well please.

MOOD ENHANCERS:
"Poison," *Rancid* by Rancid

SKILLS USED:
Basic crochet (see page 145)
Basic sewing
Seamless single crochet method (see *Educate Thyself: Crochet,* page 156)

MATERIALS AND TOOLS:
Apothecary Tote
4 skeins (120 yards or 108 meters ea) Lily Sugar 'n Cream cotton yarn color 00002 Black
Yarn for embroidery: lime green, light blue, white, and red

I [skull] Trouble Tote
3 skeins (120 yards or 108 meters ea) Lily Sugar 'n Cream cotton yarn color 00095 Red
4 skeins (120 yards or 108 meters ea) Lily Sugar 'n Cream cotton yarn color 00002 Black
Yarn for embroidery: white

Both
US H/8 (5mm) crochet hook
Yarn needle
13" × 31" (33cm × 79cm) piece of fabric for lining 12" × 13½" (30cm × 34cm) bag [for a different size bag, fabric should be (length of bag) + 1" (2.5cm) × [(height of bag)×2] + 4" (10cm)]
Scissors
Pins
Thread
Sewing needle
Sewing machine (optional)
Snap (optional)

BY ALICE MERLINO

GAUGE:
15 sc × 18 rows = 4" (10cm)

SPECIAL STITCH:
Deep Single Crochet (deep-sc)
Insert hook below next st 1 row down, yo, draw loop through and up to height of current row, yo, draw through both loops on hook.

FINISHED SIZE:
12" × 13½" (30cm × 34cm), exclusive of handles

NOTES:
The bag is worked in horizontal rows around the bag, back and forth, with the last stitch slip stitched to the first stitch of the row.

Apothecary Tote:

With black yarn:

Foundation Row: Ch 45.

Round 1: Sc twice in top bar of 2nd ch from hook, sc in top bar of each ch across to last ch, sc twice in top bar of last ch, ch 1. Rotate piece so the last ch of the foundation row is now on the right edge of the piece, sc twice in bottom bar of last ch of foundation row. Sc in bottom bar of each ch across to first ch of foundation row, sc twice in bottom bar of first ch of foundation row, sl st into first sc of row, ch 1, turn clockwise. [93 sts, plus sl st]

Round 2: Sc in sl st of previous row, sc in next 46 sc, sc in top of ch, sc in next 45 sc, sl st into first sc of row, ch 1, turn clockwise. [93 sts, plus sl st]

Rounds 3–61: Deep-sc, sc in each sc around, sl st into first sc of row, ch 1, turn clockwise. [93 sts, plus sl st]

Fasten off, weave in ends.

I [Skull] Trouble Tote:

Follow instructions for Apothecary Tote through Round 12.

Round 13: Deep-sc, sc in each sc around, insert hook into first sc of row, yo using red and sl st into first sc of row, ch 1, turn clockwise. [93 sts, plus sl st]

Repeat instructions for Rounds 3–13, alternating between black and red. You will have thirteen rows of black, twelve red, twelve black, twelve red, twelve black, for a total of 61 rows.

Fasten off, weave in ends.

Handles (make two per tote):

With black yarn:

Foundation Row: Ch 4.

Row 1: Sc in 2nd ch from hook and each of the next 2 ch, ch 1. [3]

Rows 2–92: Turn. Sc in each sc across, ch 1.

Without fastening off, sc up the edge of strap, 1 sc per row to the end of the strap. At the end, ch 1, sc into each st across the top, ch 1. Sc down edge of strap, 1 sc per row around the end stitch of each row. At the end of the strap, ch 1, fasten off, and weave in ends.

Assembly:

Measure in 2" (5cm) from each side of the bag to place strap ends. The strap should overlap with the bag for about 8 rows of crochet. Sew on the straps using yarn.

Embroidery:

Find the center of the bag. Using a yarn needle and yarn, stitch the design as charted. Knot and weave in ends. For the Apothecary Tote, double the long stitches of the bones so they look thicker.

Lining:

Fold the lining in half so the 13" (33cm) edges are together. Sew along each side to form a pouch, leaving a ½" (13mm) seam allowance. Press the seams open. Fold down the top of the lining 1" (2.5cm), then another 1" (2.5cm), enclosing the raw edges of the fabric in the fold. Sew around the edge, ½" (13mm) from the top.

Measure to the center of the lining and sew in a snap using the top seam as a guide. Pin the lining into the tote, using the top of a crochet row as a guide. Using thread and a needle, sew the lining into the bag.

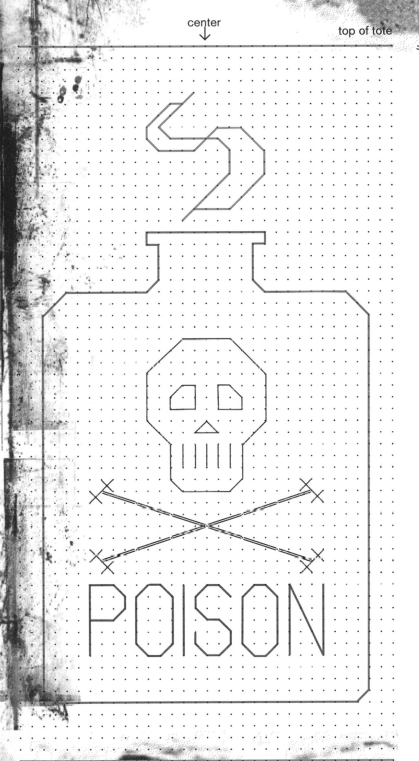

Designer bio:

Growing up in the Midwest, I was inspired and encouraged by an industrious and creative family: painters, sewers, wood carvers, potters, knitters, singers, crocheters, and all-around crafters. I've always enjoyed the process of creating and the satisfaction of doing things myself. Now I live in Philadelphia with my husband, a talented photographer, musician, and writer.

Although I've tried just about everything, crochet is my mainstay. I love its rhythm and graceful monotony. The idea that one long string can turn into a handbag seems like magic. No matter how long I've been doing it, crochet always presents me with new challenges.

My newest favorite craft is hand sewing felt stuffies. I have a growing collection of quirky Japanese craft books full of patterns for super-cute animals. It's simple and inexpensive, but the results are completely adorable. It takes only a couple hours to hand sew a stuffie, so it's perfect for crafters like me who have limited time.

I owe my current enthusiasm for crafting to the Web. I started my blog at www.futurogirl.com to connect with all the cool crafters I discovered online. There is no better place to find inspiration and share your projects. Thanks to the current popularity of crafting, the old world of staid, traditional craft books and magazines has evolved into a global, collaborative community bursting with inventive, edgy, and highly personal projects.

71

More Legal Than Drinking Blood Cordial

*

3 cups sugar
3 cups vodka
2 lbs frozen raspberries

In a large jar, stir together warmed vodka and sugar until mostly dissolved. Place raspberries in the jar, cover, and store in a cool, dark place. Stir it daily for about three weeks. Serve in lieu of blood at your sacrificial meals.

There's No Funny Way to Say Meatballs

1 medium sized jar of marinara sauce
1 12 oz jar grape jelly
2 spoons (you choose the size) horseradish
Big bag of frozen meatballs

Cook meatballs according to package directions or—gasp—make your own little balls of meat. Mix marinara, grape jelly, and horseradish. Place sauce and balls in a slow cooker. Heat well and serve with tiny toothpicks.

Hellfire Heartburn Chickpea Soup

2–2½ cups dry chickpeas (garbanzo beans)
6 cups filtered water
2 teaspoons salt (or to taste)
1 teaspoon black pepper (or to taste)
1 envelope (¹⁄₁₆ oz.) Vigo Flavoring and Coloring
½ green pepper, chopped
1 clove garlic, peeled and minced
½ can of tomato paste
2 links chorizo
1 potato, cut into 1″ (3cm) pieces

In a large bowl, soak chickpeas overnight in cold water. The bowl should be large enough to cover the chickpeas with 1–2″ (3–4cm) of water. The next day, discard soaking water.

In a large pot, combine chickpeas, water, salt, pepper, Vigo seasoning, green pepper, garlic, and tomato paste. Bring to a boil and reduce to a simmer. Meanwhile, in a small frying pan, fry chorizo over medium heat until fully cooked. Drain off fat, let cool, and slice into rounds. Add to pot. Simmer on very low heat for 4 hours or until chickpeas are tender. Add potato and simmer for 15 minutes longer.

Makes two hearty servings. Recipe doubles beautifully and is just as tasty without the chorizo for you vegetarians, though you might want to add ¼ teaspoon cayenne pepper.

3

CARRION

BY CAROL VENTURA

Ancient Egyptians, Native Americans, and Zoroastrians hold vultures in high esteem, but in much of Western culture vultures don't get the respect they deserve. This felted tapestry crochet purse is a cylindrical basket with a strap. First, the flat spiral base is crocheted, then when the diameter of the base is no longer increased, the edges of the spiral move upward to form the sides. No seams! No sewing! The bottom, sides, and strap are all one piece. Tapestry crochet differs from ordinary crochet in its texture, tension, and method of manipulating colors. Two or more yarns are single crocheted at the same time to create intricate or simple motifs. One yarn is carried while another is worked over it. This method provides flexibility and portability of crochet, but the finished pieces appear woven.

MOOD ENHANCERS:

"All Dead, All Dead," *News of the World* by Queen

SKILLS USED:

Basic crochet (see page 145)
Tapestry crochet (see page 152)
Basic sewing

NOTES:

Do not join rounds unless otherwise noted. Numbers in [ ] indicate the number of stitches in that row.

MATERIALS AND TOOLS:

3 balls (109 yards or 98 meters ea) Rowan Scottish Tweed Chunky 100% wool yarn in color Porridge (MC)
2 balls (109 yards or 98 meters ea) Rowan Scottish Tweed Chunky 100% wool yarn in color Midnight (CC)
US N/15 (10mm) hook
Stitch marker

GAUGE (BEFORE FELTING):

10 tc × 9 rows – 4" (10cm)

SPECIAL STITCH:

Tapestry crochet (TC)
To do a tapestry crochet stitch, colors are switched while 2 loops are still on the hook; yarn over with the next color and pull it through the loops to prepare for the tapestry crochet stitch. The tapestry crochet stitches used in this bag are all single crochet.

FINISHED SIZE:

13" × 11½" (33cm × 29cm) without the handle
35" (89cm) long handle

Size before felting:
19" × 12" (48cm × 30cm) without the handle

Bag

With MC:

Foundation Round: Leave an 8" (20cm) tail, ch 4, sl st into 1st ch to form a ring. Sc 6 times into the ring while carrying the tail of the yarn. Slip a stitch marker into the last st of the round. Cut the carried tail flush. [6]

For Rounds 1–11, work with MC while carrying CC.

Round 1–2: Sc 2 times into each st. [24]

Round 3: *Sc 2 times into the next st, sc into the next st. Repeat from * around. [36]

Round 4: Sc into all sts in round.

Round 5: *Sc 2 times into the next st, sc into each of the next 2 sts. Repeat from * around. [48]

Round 6: *Sc 2 times into the next st, sc into each of the next 3 sts. Repeat from * around. [60]

Round 7: *Sc 2 times into the next st, sc into each of the next 4 sts. Repeat from * around. [72]

Round 8: Sc into all sts in round.

Round 9: *Sc 2 times into the next st, sc into each of the next 5 sts. Repeat from * around. [84]

Round 10: *Sc 2 times into the next st, sc into each of the next 6 sts. Repeat from * around. [96]

Sides

Round 11: sc into all sts in round.

Begin tapestry crochet:

Round 12: *Tc 6 MC, 4 CC, 14 MC. Repeat from * around.

Round 13: *Tc 7 MC, 1 CC, 16 MC. Repeat from * around.

Round 14: *tc 1 MC, 3 CC, 3 MC, 2 CC, 15 MC. Repeat from* around.

Round 15: *Tc 2 MC, 3 CC, 1 MC, 6 CC, 12 MC. Repeat from* around.

Round 16: *Tc 3 MC, 11 CC, 10 MC. Repeat from * around.

Round 17: *Tc 17 CC, 7 MC. Repeat from * around.

Round 18: *Tc 2 MC, 16 CC, 4 MC, 1 CC, 1 MC. Repeat from* around.

Round 19: *Tc 5 MC, 10 CC, 1 MC, 8 CC. Repeat from * around.

Round 20: *Tc 7 MC, 7 CC, 2 MC, 8 CC. Repeat from * around.

Round 21: *Tc 9 MC, 5 CC, 2 MC, 2 CC, 1 MC, 1 CC, 4 MC. Repeat from * around.

Round 22: *Tc 17 MC, 3 CC, 4 MC. Repeat from * around.

Repeat Rounds 11 through 22 once.

Next Round: sc all sts with MC while carrying CC. Repeat for two more rounds. Do not cut yarn.

Handles and rim:

Round 1: With MC and CC still attached to the purse, hold MC and CC together and ch 95 (add or subtract ch sts to make handle longer or shorter), sk 22 sts (this will form the ch 95 into a large loop), sc 22 with CC while carrying MC, ch 5 with MC and CC together. Lay the first half of the ch 95 loop between the rim and the chain, sk 5 sts, sc into next st with CC while carrying MC, capturing the handle, sc into next 19 sts with CC while carrying MC, ch 5 with MC and CC together. Lay the second half of the ch 95 loop between the rim and the chain, sk 5 sts, sc into next st with CC while carrying MC, capturing the handle, sc into next 21 sts with CC while carrying MC, sc into each ch in ch 95 loop with CC while carrying MC.

Round 2: While carrying MC, sc into each st around with CC, including handle. Cut the MC yarn flush, sl st with CC, cut the CC leaving a 10" (25cm) tail. Yo and pull the tail all the way through the loop. Work in the tail for 8" (20cm) to secure it.

Round 3: Turn the purse over and insert the hook under the upper two loops of the stitch where the handle chain started. Pull through a loop of CC, leaving a 4" (10cm) tail. Ch 1 with CC, sc into the same st with CC while carrying MC and CC tail, sc into each st between the ends of the handle with CC while carrying MC, sc 1 with CC while carrying MC into the st at the base of the second piece of the handle, sc into the bottom loops of each st of the handle with CC while carrying MC. Push CC and MC through the openings capturing the handle as needed.

Round 4: Sc across the rim and handle with CC while carrying MC. Push CC and MC through the openings capturing the handle as needed. At the end of the round, cut the MC flush, slip stitch with CC, cut the CC leaving a 10" (25cm) tail. Yo and pull the yarn through the loop. Work in the end for 8" (20cm) to secure it.

Felting:

Wash the purse four times, or until bag reaches desired size, in a washing machine set to medium water level with 2 tablespoons of mild soap (Ivory Dishwashing Liquid works great). Let the bag air dry, then iron it with a steam iron. You may wish to shave it with a pair of clippers to reduce fuzziness.

Designer bio:

Carol Ventura discovered tapestry crochet in Guatemala in the 1970s when she was a Peace Corps volunteer there. Since then, she developed special WYSIWYG tapestry crochet graph papers and continues to research tapestry crochet around the world. Her early work featured tapestry crochet portraits, but the obsession du jour is felted tapestry crochet.

To help spread the excitement about this versatile technique, Carol teaches tapestry crochet at international conferences and designs projects for numerous publications, including *Piecework, Bead & Button, Crochet World* and *Simply Creative Crochet*. Carol hopes to inspire you free-spirited AntiCrafters to break out of her structured approach, though, and go nuts with tapestry crochet! As a Professor of Art History at Tennessee Technological University, she is exposed to amazing art and crafts from around the world that often influence her work. Check out http://iweb.tntech.edu/cventura/ for more about Carol.

THE WHILAMEENAS

BY PD CAGLIASTRO

Ahh, remember those lyrics….

With a friend to call my own, I'll never be alone.
—Michael Jackson, "Ben"

These two little Whilameenas will always have each other, but sadly enough will never be able to look each other in the eye and see each other's smile. Sweet and sad, but gentle and loving, they should be made for the person you could never imagine living without.

MOOD ENHANCERS:

Willard (1971, rated PG); *Ben* (1972, rated PG); *Willard* (2003, remake, rated PG-13)

SKILLS USED:

Basic crochet (see page 145)

MATERIALS AND TOOLS:

A few ounces of sport weight wool.
Size C/2 (2.75mm) or D/3 (3.25mm) crochet hook (choose which one gives you a tighter stitch)
A yard of contrasting sport-weight wool (face and whiskers)
Yarn needle
Polyester fiberfill

NOTES:

The Whilameenas will stand by themselves if you make the fabric of the crochet tight. Remember when turning to make your turning chain. It is important to make the piece even. Forgetting the turning chain causes distortion in the work. I have added the instruction to ch where there are short rows.

Do not trim the yarn tails off of any of the pieces until the Whilameenas are assembled. The yarn tails will be used to sew the pieces together.

Arms (make four):

Foundation Row: Ch 10.
Rows 1: Sc in second ch from hook, sc in each ch across.
Rows 2–3: Turn. Ch 1. Sc in each st across.
Fasten off, leaving at least a 6" (15cm) tail.
Fold the arm in half the long way (pin it if it feels too tiny to hold and sew.) Using the yarn needle and the remaining yarn tail, whip stitch the arm closed. Tie off and leave a yarn tail for sewing.

Legs (make two):

Foundation Row: Ch 25.
Rows 1: Sc in second ch from hook, sc in each ch across.
Rows 2–5: Turn. Ch 1. Sc in each st across.
Fasten off, leaving at least an 8" (20cm) tail.
Fold the leg in half the long way (pin it if it feels too tiny to hold and sew). Using the yarn needle and the remaining yarn tail, whip stitch the leg closed, leaving the last 5 stitches open. This flat part will be sewn on as the thigh to the body. Tie off and leave yarn tail for sewing.

Ears (make three):

Foundation Row: Ch 5.
Row 1: Sc in second ch from hook, sc in next 3 ch, 2 sc in last ch. Working around foundation chain to the opposite side, sc 3, sc 2 times into the next st.
Row 2–5: Turn. Ch1, sk 1, sc in next 4 sts.
Fasten off, leaving at least a 5" (13cm) tail.

Tail:

Foundation Row: Ch 45.

Row 1: Sc in second ch from hook, sc in each ch across.

Row 2: Turn. Ch 1. Sc in each st across.

Row 3: Turn. Ch 1. Sc in next 40 sts.

Row 4: Turn. Ch 1, sk 1, sc in each st across.

Row 5: Turn. Ch 1. Sc in next 35 sts.

Row 6: Turn. Ch 1, sk 1, sc in each st across.

Row 7: Turn. Sc into the next 27 sts.

Row 8: Turn. Ch 1, sk 1, sc in each st across.

Row 9: Turn. Ch 1. Sc in next 20 sts.

Row 10: Turn. Ch 1, sk 1, sc in each st across.

Fasten off, leaving at least a 10" (25cm) tail.

Fold the tail in half the long way (pin it if it feels too tiny to hold and sew). Using the yarn needle and the remaining yarn tail, whip stitch the tail closed, leaving the last 5 stitches on the wider part of the tail open. This flat part will be sewn under the body. Tie off and leave yarn tail for sewing.

Stuff the wider end of the tail with fiberfill until it is stiff.

Heads:

Foundation Round: Ch 3, sl st into first ch to form a ring, sc 4 times into ring. [4]

Working in a spiral, *sc in next 2 sts, 2 sc in next st. Repeat from * until there are 28 sts.

Place marker to mark the beginning of the round.

Next Round: Sc into each st around. Repeat this round twice more. Begin working short rows:

Row 1: Turn. Ch 1, sk 1, sc into the next 18 sts.

Row 2: Turn. Ch 1, sk 1, sc into the next 14 sts.

Row 3: Turn. Ch 1, sk 1, sc into the next 11 sts.

Next Round: Turn. Ch 1, sc into each st in the round, closing any holes created by the short rows by picking up sts and working them together with the following st so the number of sts does not increase. The entire round should have 28 sts.

Next Round: Sc into the next 22 sts, ch 6 (this makes the hole for stuffing), sk 6, sc into next st.

Next Round: Sc into each st in the round. Repeat this round two more times.

Working in a spiral, *sc into the next 2 sts, dec. Repeat from * until 4 sts remain.

Next Round: Sc into all sts.

Cut the yarn leaving a yarn tail. To fasten off, thread your needle with the yarn tail, pass the needle through the last 4 sts and drawstring them closed. Tie off the yarn inside of the head.

Stuff firmly with fiberfill. Do not close the hole.

Body:

Foundation Round: Ch 5, sl st into first ch to form a ring. Sc 6 times into the ring.

Working in a spiral, *sc into the next 2 sts, sc 2 times into the next st. Repeat from * until there are 32 sts. Place marker to mark beginning of round.

Next Round: Sc into each st around. Repeat this round five more times. Begin working short rows to form a belly.

Row 1: Turn. Ch 1, sk 1, sc into the next 18 sts.

Row 2: Turn. Ch 1, sk 1, sc into the next 16 sts.

Row 3: Turn. Ch 1, sk 1, sc into the next 14 sts.

Row 4: Turn. Ch 1, sk 1, sc into the next 11 sts.

Row 5: Turn. Ch 1, sk 1, sc into the next 18 sts.

Next Round: Turn. Ch 1, sc into each st in the round, closing any holes created by the short rows by picking up sts and working them together with the following st so the number of sts does not increase. The entire round should have 32 stitches.

Next Round: Sc into each st around. Repeat this round two more times.

Next Round: Sc into all sts until you are opposite the furthest point out of the belly. Begin working short rows to form the butt.

Row 1: Sc into the next 6 sts.

Row 2: Turn. Ch 1, sk 1, sc into the next 7 sts.

Row 3: Turn. Ch 1, sk 1, sc into the next 8 sts.

Row 4: Turn. Ch 1, sk 1, sc into the next 8 sts.

Next Round: Turn. Ch 1, sc into each st in the round, closing any holes created by the short rows by picking up sts and working them together with the following st so the number of sts does not increase. The entire round should have 32 stitches.

Next Round: Sc into each st around. Repeat this round once more.

Stuff firmly before this next instruction. With stuffing in place, work in a spiral, *sc into the next 2 sts, dec. Repeat from * until 16 sts remain.

Next Round: Dec around until 8 sts remain.

Make sure the stuffing is tight and the body is firm. Cut the yarn leaving a yarn tail. To fasten off, thread your needle with the yarn tail, pass the needle through the last 8 sts and drawstring it closed. Tie off.

Assembly:

With the head opening vertical, push the neck into the head at the base of the opening. Pose the head with the attitude you feel is right for your Whilameenas, and use a yarn needle to sew the head to the body. Close up the rest of the opening by drawing the two heads together with the stitching. This will make the heads face each other a bit, and will conceal the neck top. Stitch down the base of the back of the head a bit. The wide part of the head is the true back, as these rats are conjoined at the side and part of the back of their heads.

Sew the open parts of the legs flat onto the outer sides of the body, just at the ends of the short rows that create the belly. Sew the arms in two sets, giving each rat her own two arms. Sew the flat open part of the tail under the body.

To attach the ears to the head, thread your needle with the yarn tail, pass the needle through the stitches along the flat end of the ear, and drawstring it a bit. Fold the ends over and sew down. This will cause the top of the ear to round over. Sew the ears on by putting two in the back and one in the center front.

Using your contrast thread and a yarn needle, embroider the eyes by whip stitching around the same spot several times. Take your time to decide where the eyes should be on your Whilameenas. Do the same type of process for the noses, continue until thick, and then make one more stitch below the nose for the mouth.

Fold the contrast yarn three times over 2" (5cm). Push your crochet hook through the face where you want to place the whiskers, and pull the folded whiskers (now 6-ply) through the face. Cut the loops open.

Love your Whilameenas—because somebody has to . . . .

Designer bio:

PD Cagliastro's couture hand knit one of a-kind dresses, gowns, and accessories sell in Madison Avenue Boutiques in New York. She is launching a couture coat line for Fall 2007. Her work has been televised in shows such as *Rockstar Super Nova*, a television show featuring Tommy Lee and Dave Navarro. She owned and originated The Knitting Salon, a knitting store/school and coffee bar that opened in 1999. PD lives in Manhattan's Financial District with her fantastic seven-year-old daughter Mahgdalen, her delightful British husband, David, and her large black hybrid bird, the craven Zaedoc.

81

A Gathering of Souls: Throw an Anticrafty Party

A time comes in the lives of sinister crafters when they realize they need to reaffirm how much they hate other people. Perhaps the perfect way to attain this enlightenment is to throw a party. Throwing a party is not as simple as inviting over a few people and slapping some food on the coffee table—it is an art. One you probably cannot learn, but we will labor to teach you anyway. We've got to earn our keep on this book somehow!

Theme

The first step in hosting a party is to decide what kind of party it will be. There are many options, but for the purposes of space, we will say simply this: Go with your strengths. And with your fondue pot. You can't go wrong with fondue. Once you decide which theme will be your own, you must pick out décor and music to suit the mood you would like to create.

Décor

Décor is very personal. If you are afraid of strangulation, you may wish to avoid streamers or balloons with long strings. Go instead with confetti and an animatronic centerpiece (choose something seasonal). Of course, you could always go with candles. Lots of candles. If you're having a fondue party—well!—it practically decorates itself, as melted cheese will fling itself off your fork at unexpected intervals. Not only is it pretty, it can be a fun party game to avoid the scalding goo.

Music

Music is the heartbeat that keeps a party alive. Will your party have the circulation of a twenty-year-old vegan? Or will it die a cholesterol-induced death? Only you can prevent celebratory heart disease. Your music selections will determine the mood of your guests, and thusly how long they will stick around and look at your stuff. So choose something good, but not too good.

Sustenance

If for no other reason, you should throw a party to expose others to your cooking and extort favors from them when they are high on carbs. Throughout the book you will find our favorite recipes, so even the least talented chef can hold a fête to make her mama shudder.

The Holy Host(ess)

Ignore everything we've said previously, because the most important part of a good party is you. Man, that's saptastic, but it's true. Without a good host or hostess, even the best theme, décor, food, and music will be pointless. Your duties will be to make sure the party stays alive between song changes, awkward silences, and Aunt Mary puking up Zombies in the corner. Make sure you are up to the task before sending out invitations, otherwise no one will come the next time you need to remember why you hate people.

Party Favors

Partygoers are selfish and they expect more than just the chance to spend time with you. They want something to take home with them as well, other than loose change they stole from discarded purses and coats in the spare room. This means party favors.

Party favors can be as simple as papier-mâché sugar skulls that you spent weeks making, or as complicated as a few pieces of extra-dark chocolate in a tiny paper bag. Consider illustrated Bible tracts that are widely available for download on the Internet—not only will you amuse your guests with your ironic flair, that way you'll rack up God points (in case it turns out we've all been terribly, terribly wrong).

If you are hosting the "No really, I'm a vampire!" set, consider a homemade blood-red cordial in a tiny jar (see page 73). They will feel validated, and you will feel superior. But don't forget, a fondue party practically favors itself, as your guests will steal the matching fondue forks. Which are, of course, practically impossible to replace.

After the Gathering

When you finally roll the last drunk off the balcony, your party is over. Chances are this is a time of mixed emotions for you. Sure, you hosted the gathering of the year, so you should be proud, but now you are faced with a messy dwelling and no one to help you clean up. If you have small children, they can be put to work in the morning, unless they are alcoholics, in which case they would probably just skim off the remaining booze, and that should not be encouraged. An easier, but illegal, option is arson.

Don't forget that after acting as a charming hostess or host, you've earned the right to collapse onto the couch and worry about cleaning when the discarded food starts to talk back. We're sure it will all get cleaned up sometime. Later. For now, my dear, you deserve a rest.

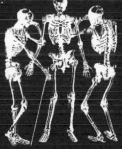

Renée's Great-Aunt Mildred is recorded in history as the world's first seamstress. After an argument with her drunken husband—folklore says the argument was over a garment that had fallen apart at its glued seams (the only way that garments had been constructed since the beginning of time)—Aunt Mildred decided she would show her loose-lipped husband a thing or two. She invented sewing and, with a needle and thread, sewed the man into a low-thread-count bedsheet. When he awoke, hung over, he was surprised to find himself in an unbreakable bag! When he complained, she beat him to death with a frying pan. Later, lazy copycats would invent a sewing machine. A sewing machine can sew three-hundred stitches per second. Which means, with the help of Christopher Lloyd, you too can travel back in time and narrowly avoid sleeping with your mother. It also means if you puncture yourself, you will bleed to death in seventy six hours unless you seek immediate medical attention—or Christopher Lloyd.

BAD EGGS

BY ALICE MERLINO

Bad Eggs are my antidote for the perky pastels and fluffy animal babies of the hop-hop-hoppiest time of the year. Balance out your Easter basket with the mordantly cute pastel decoy eggs. One features a chick holding an eye by the optical nerve and a basket full of eyes. Or maybe you prefer the severed bunny head whose arterial blood-spurting body is on the reverse. For the less subtle, create the fully bad black eggs in either the evil eye or hellfire designs. No matter which bad eggs you make, you will be doing your part to keep the universe in check. Who knows what catastrophes an irresponsible overload of snuggly cuteness could cause?

NOTES:

When assembling the egg pieces, use a 26" (66cm) piece of embroidery floss. This ensures that you'll be able to go up one edge of the egg and down the other and the knots will always be at the bottom edge of the egg.

MOOD ENHANCERS:

Green Eggs and Ham by Dr. Seuss

SKILLS USED:

Basic sewing
Basic embroidery
Felt sewing method (see *Educate Thyself: Sewing,* page 156)

MATERIALS AND TOOLS:

Craft felt in assorted colors (see instructions for color guidance)
6-strand embroidery floss in assorted colors (see instructions)
Polyfill
Sequins (see instructions)
Seed beads (see instructions)
1" (2.5cm) washer for each egg
Sewing needle
Scissors
Tracing pencil or pen
Pins

Hallowed Counsel

Thread a bunch of needles beforehand, which makes it easier to keep working. If you have curious cats or little children, you can hide the pincushion under a bowl to keep from tempting them with dangling threads.

—Andrea Stern

A boring pattern doesn't have to stay boring! Try remaking that flirty pink summer dress in black vinyl. Also, you can: change the colors in afghans and other projects to make them more suitable for your lair; change the words in cross-stitch (à la *Subversive Cross Stitch*); sew scars, fangs, and weird eyeballs on cuddly teddy bears, etc.

—Alice Merlino

HEADLESS BUNNY EGG:

Felt: Violet, White, Red
Floss: White, Black, Red, Pink, Violet

1. Using the template (see page 90) as a guide, cut out four egg pieces and one bottom circle from violet felt. Cut out one bunny head, two bunny ears, one bunny body, and one bone (small rectangle) from white felt. Cut out one bloody hole from red felt.

2. Pin the bunny body onto one egg piece with the bottom of the bunny body 1" (2.5cm) from the bottom of the egg piece. Sew on the body using white floss. Using white floss, backstitch the bunny leg outline onto the body. Create a fluffy tail by embroidering white floss loops at the back bottom of the bunny body.

3. Sew on bloody hole at the top left of the bunny body using red floss. Sew on the bone so it appears to be sticking out of the bloody hole. Embroider blood drips and arterial spray using red floss.

4. Pin the bunny head on a different egg piece with the bottom edge of the bunny head 1" (2.5cm) from the bottom of the egg piece. Leave space to the left of the bunny head for the ears. Sew on bunny head using white floss.

5. Place the ears so the bottom ear lies horizontally and the top ear angles downward and covers the bottom ear. Make sure the base of each ear overlaps the head a little. Attach the ears using long stitches in pink floss.

6. Add the X eyes, French knot nose, and bunny mouth using black floss. Add a line of red floss at the base of the head (right edge) and a blood drip coming from the base of the head using a backstitch and a French knot in red floss.

7. Pin the bunny body egg piece to a blank egg piece, wrong sides together. Sew along the edge from the bottom of the egg to the top using violet floss.

8. Pin the bunny head egg piece to the other edge of the blank egg piece, wrong sides together. Sew along the edge from top to bottom using violet floss.

9. Pin the remaining blank egg piece to the bunny head and bunny body pieces, wrong sides together, and sew along both edges using violet floss.

10. Use polyfil to stuff the egg most of the way. Pin the bottom to the egg and sew halfway around the opening using violet floss.

11. Finish stuffing the egg and place a 1" (2.5cm) washer on the bottom of the egg. Finish sewing the bottom on the egg.

EYEPLUCKING CHICK EGG

Felt: Pink, Yellow, Orange, Brown, Green
Floss: Ecru, Black, Green, Yellow, Orange, Red, Pink
Sequins: White
Seed beads: Black

1. Using the template as a guide, cut out four egg pieces and one bottom circle from pink felt. Cut out one chick head and one chick body from yellow felt. Cut out one chick beak from orange felt. Cut out one basket interior from green felt. Cut out one basket and one basket handle from brown felt.

2. Layer the chick body and head on an egg piece with the bottom of the chick's body 1" (2.5cm) from the bottom of the egg piece. Sew on the chick body and head using yellow floss.

3. Using orange floss, sew on the chick's beak along the top of the triangle so the bottom is loose. Also using orange floss, embroider the chick legs under the chick body.

4. Using black floss, attach two black seed beads as eyes. Using red floss, embroider an optical nerve so it looks like it's being held in the chick's mouth. Make the left side pointed and the right side thicker.

5. On the thick end of the optical nerve, attach a white sequin using black floss and a black seed bead, forming an eye. Add three eyelashes to the eye with black floss. (Note: While it is true that eyes plucked from bodies by chicks would not have eyelashes, it's much funnier that way.)

6. Layer the basket interior and the basket on a different egg piece with the bottom edge of the basket 1" (2.5cm) from the bottom of the egg piece. Sew around the top of the basket interior with green floss. Using ecru floss, sew a crosshatch pattern on the basket.

7. Place the basket handle so it arches over the basket. Attach by couching it in ecru floss.

8. Attach white sequins to the basket interior using black floss and black seed beads. Add three black floss lashes to each eye. Tuck some of the white sequins at the bottom of the basket interior under the basket so they appear to be inside the basket.

9. Add the X eyes, French knot nose, and bunny mouth using black floss.

10. Pin the chick egg piece to a blank egg piece, wrong sides together, and sew along the edge, from bottom to top, using pink floss.

11. Pin the basket egg piece to the other edge of the blank egg piece, wrong sides together. Sew along the edge, from top to bottom, using pink floss.

12. Pin the remaining blank egg piece to the chick and basket pieces, wrong sides together. Sew along the edges using pink floss.

13. Stuff the egg most of the way, pin the bottom to the egg and sew halfway around using pink floss.

14. Finish stuffing the egg and place a 1" (2.5cm) washer on the inside bottom of the egg. Finish sewing the bottom on the egg.

EVIL EYE EGG
Felt: Black
Floss: Green, Yellow, Red, Orange, Blue, Black
Sequins: Round White and Blue; Green, Orange, and Red Stars
Seed beads: Blue, Green, Orange, Red, Black

1. Using the template as a guide, cut out four egg pieces, one bottom circle, and one eye shape from black felt.

2. Pin the eye shape to one of the black felt egg pieces and use as guide to backstitch the eye shape in blue floss. Remove the pattern piece and backstitch the eyelid following the curve of the eye.

3. Add five yellow lashes above the eye and three below.

4. Attach a white sequin layered with a blue star-shaped sequin and a black seed bead in the middle of the eye.

5. Repeat Steps 2–4 for each egg piece with orange, green, and red floss, using orange, green, and red star sequins.

6. Pin the blue eye and orange eye egg pieces together, wrong sides together. Sew along the edge using black floss.

7. Pin the green eye piece to the orange eye egg piece, wrong sides together. Sew along the edge using black floss.

8. Pin the red eye egg piece to the green eye and blue eye egg pieces, wrong sides together. Sew along the edges using black floss.

9. Stuff egg most of the way.

10. Pin the bottom to the egg and sew halfway around using black floss.

11. Finish stuffing the egg and place a 1" (2.5cm) washer on the bottom inside of the egg. Finish sewing the bottom on the egg.

HELLFIRE EGG
Felt: Black
Floss: Light Yellow, Orange Yellow, Orange, Red, Black

1. Using the template as a guide, cut out four egg pieces and one bottom circle from black felt.

2. Place the pattern piece on one of the black felt egg pieces and mark the placement of the top tick marks on the pattern piece using pins. With light yellow floss and using a backstitch, embroider the peaks of the flame so the right and left edges of the flame start and end at the pins.

3. Place the pattern piece on the same black felt egg piece and use pins to mark the placement of the middle tick marks on the pattern piece. With orange yellow floss and using a backstitch, embroider the peaks of the flame following the lines of the light yellow stitching.

4. Place the pattern piece on the same black felt egg piece and use pins to mark the placement of the bottom tick marks on the pattern piece. With orange floss and using a backstitch, embroider the peaks of the flame following the lines of the orange yellow stitching.

5. With red floss and using a backstitch, embroider the peaks of the flame following the lines of the orange stitching. Instead of stopping at the edges, continue around the bottom edge of the egg piece to make a rounded bottom for the flame.

6. Repeat Steps 2–4 on each egg piece. I alternated three-point and two-point flames on my egg pieces.

7. Pin two egg pieces together, wrong sides together. Sew along the edge using black floss.

8. Pin a third egg piece to the two connected egg pieces, wrong sides together. Sew along the edge using black floss.

9. Pin the forth egg piece to the first and third egg pieces, wrong sides togother, and sew along the edges using black floss.

10. Using the appropriate color of floss, connect the flame lines between the egg pieces.

11. Stuff the egg most of the way. Pin the bottom to the egg and sew halfway around using black floss.

12. Finish stuffing the egg and place a 1" (2.5cm) washer on the bottom of the egg. Finish sewing the bottom on the egg.

Designer bio:
To read about Alice, see page 71.

CHICK   BASKET

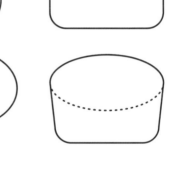

EGG BOTTOM

EGG SIDE

BUNNY

TEMPLATES ARE ACTUAL SIZE.

THREE OWLS

BY ALICE MERLINO

Scared of the dark? Have mice in the house? Need someone to keep the clown dolls in check? Then all you need to do is stitch up a parliament of owls to watch over you. Make these palm-sized, nocturnal birds of prey using felt and embroidery floss. They are designed to stand up on their own, or you can omit the bottom pattern piece and make them flat. Add a loop of string to turn them into an ornament or glue a magnet on the back so they can protect the take-out menus on the fridge.

MOOD ENHANCERS:

Explore owls on TV and in the movies: *Twin Peaks* (not what they seem; TV); *Blade Runner* (replicant; 1982, rated R); *Clash of the Titans* (clockwork; 1981, rated PG)

SKILLS USED:

Basic sewing
Basic embroidery
Felt sewing method (see *Educate Thyself: Sewing*, on page 156)

MATERIALS AND TOOLS:

Craft felt in assorted colors (see instructions for color guidance)
6-strand embroidery floss in assorted colors (see instructions)
Fiberfill
Plastic beads
1" (2.5cm) washer
Sewing needle
Scissors
Tracing pencil or pen
Pins

Hallowed Counsel

Protect your fabric scissors by using them only on fabric. Using them on paper will cause them to dull much more quickly.

—Renée

LARGE OWL:

Felt: Charcoal, Gray
Floss: Light Gray, Dark Gray, Red, Black

1. Using the template (page 94) as a guide, cut out two body pieces, one beak, and one bottom circle from charcoal felt. Cut out one face piece from gray felt.

2. Place the face piece on the front body piece ¹⁄₁₆" (2mm) from the top of the front body piece. Sew the face to body around the sides and bottom edge using light gray floss. Leave the top edge open.

3. Place the beak piece on top of the face matching the top of the beak to the front body piece. Sew the beak to the face using dark gray floss. Sew all edges except for the top edge.

4. Cut out the guide pattern piece and cut out the eye circles. Place the guide over the face of the owl and pin in place. Use the tick marks on the outside of the eye circles on the guide to embroider the burst eyes in red floss.

5. Add the front and back feathers to the body pieces using black floss in the fly stitch.

6. Pin the front body piece to the back body pieces, wrong sides together. Stitch the sides and top together using dark gray floss. When stitching the top, be sure to catch the beak and both body pieces so they close to hide the face piece.

7. Stuff the owl three-quarter full with fiberfill.

8. Pin on bottom circle and sew halfway around using dark gray floss.

9. Finish filling the owl with plastic beads and put a 1" (2.5cm) washer on the bottom. The beads and the washer add weight to keep the owl standing. The washer creates a flat bottom surface for the owl.

10. Finish sewing on the bottom circle.

MEDIUM OWL:

Felt: Charcoal, Red
Floss: White, Black, Dark Gray, Red

1. Using the template as a guide, cut out one body piece and one beak from red felt. Cut out one body piece, one bottom circle, and one face piece from charcoal felt.

2. Place the face piece on the front body piece ¹⁄₁₆" (2mm) from the top of the front body piece. Sew the face to the body around the sides and bottom edge using black floss. Leave the top edge open.

3. Place the beak piece on top of the face matching the top of the beak to the underlying front body piece. Sew the beak to the face using red floss. Sew all edges except for the top edge.

4. Cut out the guide pattern piece. Place the guide over the face of the owl and pin in place. Embroider the outline of the eyes in white floss, using the guide. Remove the guide and embroider a swirl inside each eye, using white floss.

5. Add feathers to the front of the owl using short straight stitches in gray floss.

6. Pin the front body piece to the back body piece, wrong sides together. Stitch the sides and top together using red floss. When stitching the top, be sure to catch the beak and both body pieces so they close to hide the edge of the face piece.

7–10. See steps 7–10 from Large Owl. Use red floss to secure bottom piece.

SMALL OWL:

Felt: Black, White, Charcoal
Floss: Black, Gray, Red

1. Using the template as a guide, cut out two body pieces and one bottom circle from black felt. Cut out one face piece from white felt. Cut out one beak from charcoal felt.

2. Blanket-stitch the face to the front body using gray floss.

3. Sew the beak to the front body piece using gray floss.

4. Embroider the eyes using French knots in red floss. You can use the face pattern piece as a guide for placement of the eyes.

5. Using the guide pattern piece, add an arc of red running stitch on the right and left sides of the owl. Add a second arc of backstitch under the first one.

6. Pin the front body piece to the back body piece, wrong sides together. Stitch the sides and top together using black floss.

7–10. See steps 7–10 from Large Owl. Use black floss to secure bottom piece.

Designer bio:

To read about Alice, see page 71.

MEDIUM

guide

SMALL

guide

bottom circle

ENLARGE TEMPLATES TO 133%.

LARGE

guide

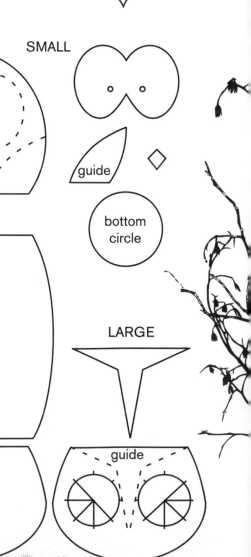

WHEEL OF THE YEAR

BY SARAH HOOD

This skirt has no front or back; I suggest whatever holiday is closest be worn in the front. It is a fairly time-intensive project, what with all the copying, cutting, ironing, cutting, ironing, cutting, sewing, ironing, sewing, and ironing to be done, but it's well worth it in the end. It is best if all fabrics are the same type of material. You are likely to find the widest range of color choices in a lightweight cotton.

MOOD ENHANCERS:

Pagan Poetry by Bjork

SKILLS USED:

Basic sewing

Appliqué

MATERIALS AND TOOLS:

Quantities for fabric based on a 45" (114cm) width.

½ yard each (46cm) of fabric in black, green, pale green, bright yellow, pale yellow, white, rust orange, and maroon

⅛ yard (11cm) red fabric

¼ yard (23cm) light brown fabric

1 yard (91cm) dark brown fabric

1 yard (91cm) of Therm O Web HEATnBOND Lite

Thread in white, silver, yellow ochre, green, light green, red, and dark brown (If you do not have a thread collection to draw on, you can select only a few colors to use, but one of them should be brown.)

¾" (2cm) wide elastic, enough to go around your waist

Scissors

Iron

Pins

Sewing machine or a needle and a ton of patience

FINISHED SIZE:

XS (up to size 6) X = 3½" (9cm) Y = 40" (102cm)

S (sizes 6-10) X = 4" (10cm) Y = 44" (112cm)

M (sizes 10-14) X = 4½" (11cm) Y = 48" (122cm)

L (sizes 14-18W) X = 5" (13cm) Y = 52" (132cm)

XL (sizes 18W-22W) X = 5½" (14cm) Y = 56" (142 cm)

XXL (size 24W-28W) X = 6" (15cm) Y = 60" (152cm)

Skirt requires:

8 Piece A rectangles in brown, [2½" × 38" (6cm × 97cm)]

8 Piece B rectangles in brown [3" × 10" (8cm × 41cm)]

1 Piece C trapezoid in each of the following colors: black, green, pale green, bright yellow, pale yellow, white, rust orange, and maroon [34" (86cm) tall, 16" (41cm) wide at the base and X wide at the top]

1 Piece D strip in brown [3½" (9cm) wide × Y tall]

NOTE:

I have allowed for ½" (13mm) seam allowances throughout this skirt. There are sixteen vertical seams in this skirt, so if you use substantially more or less than ½" (13mm) for your seams, it will affect the size of the skirt

1. Enlarge the appliqué patterns (page 99) by 400%. If you print them on cardstock it will be easier to trace them later. Cut out the patterns.

2. Wash and dry all fabric.

3. Cut all of the fabric pieces. To make sure the trapezoid pieces are symmetrical, fold them in half lengthwise and check that the edges match.

4. Cut the adhesive (with paper attached) into 8" (20cm) squares. Cut 8½" (22cm) squares of each appliqué color. Iron one adhesive piece onto the wrong side of each piece of applique fabric, as per instructions. Do not remove paper backing.

5. Place the applique symbol, black side down, onto the paper side of paper-fabric piece and trace it. Cut out the applique, then remove paper backing.

6. Center the prepared applique symbol, fabric side up, a couple of inches (or centimeters) above the wide end of the appropriate color panel (see color chart, page 103), and iron on, per adhesive instructions.

7. If you are new to sewing, don't be afraid of the machine. Locate the stitch length and stitch width adjustment knobs. Play around with them a bit on a spare piece of fabric. Set your machine on zig zag stitch, set the width of the stitch about ³⁄₃₂" (2mm) wide (does not have to be exact) and set the stitch length very short, so there is no fabric showing between stitches, but not so small that the stitches are on top of each other. Try this setting out on a scrap piece of fabric. Once you are satisfied with the settings, you are ready to appliqué. Begin with a simple symbol, such as the crescent moon. Place the fabric so most of the stitch covers the symbol fabric, and only the end is on the panel fabric. Start at a corner, and gently guide the work as needed. When you get to a sharp corner, you should stop the machine with the needle down, lift the foot, and rotate the fabric so you can begin a new line. I used a narrower stitch [about ¹⁄₁₆" (2mm) wide] for the Triskele and St. Brigit's cross symbols so the thread would not take up more space than the fabric. The St. Brigit's cross symbol has interior detailing; you can either machine stitch this, as for the appliqués, or embroider it.

8. This is a fabulous skirt, and you want it to last. To prevent the fabric from unraveling, you need to make the seams secure. To do this, set your machine to zig zag stitch, with a regularly spaced stitch length. Stitch every piece of fabric you have cut with the zig zag stitch close to the edge. Is this annoying? Yes. Does it make a difference? Unless you are working with leather or polar fleece, yes.

9. Place one Piece B on the bottom of each Piece C, right sides together. Most sewing resources advise you to pin the fabric in place prior to sewing, but this is entirely up to you. Using a straight stitch, sew these together. Leave approximately ½" (13mm) for the seam allowance. If your machine has one, use the guide on the throat plate of your sewing machine to follow the seam allowance.

10. With an iron set to the appropriate setting for your fabric, use steam and press the seams you have just sewn outwards on the wrong side of the fabric, so each side flips back onto the same color fabric.

11. Place Piece A on a join of Piece B/C, right sides together. Line the bottom edges up and sew together as for step 9. Repeat for all pieces.

12. Line up the pieces in the order of the year and sew them all together. Begin sewing with the bottom edges lined up.

13. On the bottom edge of the skirt, fold ¼" (6mm) toward the inside, then fold again. Sew this in place all around the hem with brown thread.

14. With the skirt inside out, iron all the seams you have just sewn, including the hem. Trim the tops of any pieces that are sticking up past the others. Iron Piece D in half lengthwise.

15. Measure your waist, subtract 1½" (4cm). Using this measurement, cut a piece of ¾" (2cm) elastic.

16. Cut both ends of Piece D on parallel 45° angles and sew them together to make a complete circle for the waistband. Alternatively, cut 2" (5cm) off and sew it straight. It's not as professional, but it's not a big deal.

17. Place four pins around the waistband, dividing it into four equal sections. Place three pins in the elastic, dividing it into four equal sections.

18. Place the elastic close to the ironed fold in the waistband. Anchor the elastic onto the fabric by sewing forward and reverse a couple times. Holding the fabric from both sides, stretch the elastic between the first two pins. Sew along one edge of the elastic. When you come to a pin, remove it and restretch the elastic. When you have sewn all the way around, sew the other edge of the elastic.

19. Fold the waistband so the fabric is over the elastic on both sides. Place eight pins around the waistband, dividing it into eight equal sections. Place the side of the waistband without stitching to the right side of the skirt and attach each pin to the center of the top of a Piece C.

20. Sew the waist onto the skirt. If there is any excess fabric in the skirt fabric, fold the seams over a little as you sew over them.

21. Blessed be! Put on the skirt and prance about in front of a full length mirror.

Designer bio:

Sarah Hood is a self-taught seamstress who always works from her own patterns. She is a crafting maniac, a vegan, a thrift-store junkie and a home birth midwife. She tries to use recycled, organic, or sustainable materials as much as possible. She is the co-owner of a fabulous store called ReBelle (www.rebellegirls.com) that has wonderful yarn, knitting accessories and books, recycled gift items, natural women's health, and locally handmade products. She is a Certified Professional Midwife and thinks women should explore home birth and talk to someone who has had one before they choose to have their baby in a hospital. She lives in The AntiCraft's hometown of Lexington, Kentucky.

Variation: Phases of the moon skirt

(This simple variation is considerably easier to appliqué and uses far fewer colors.)

In colors of your choosing, cut out the same fabric pieces.

Use the following symbols: new moon, waxing crescent, waxing half, waxing gibbons, full moon, waning gibbons, waning half, waning crescent. I have faith that no matter how horrible your drawing skills are, you can do this! (You can flip the waxing half, crescent, and gibbons over to get the waning ones).

Hallowed Counsel

Choose the appropriate needle for the fabric when machine sewing. When you go to buy your sewing machine needles, look very carefully at the package to make sure you are getting the right needles for either woven or knit fabric, as well as for the weight of the fabric.

—Renée

The OCD crafter says: Create a swatch binder with a note about fiber content and yardage. When planning projects, you know what you have on hand by flipping through your fabric index.

—Renée

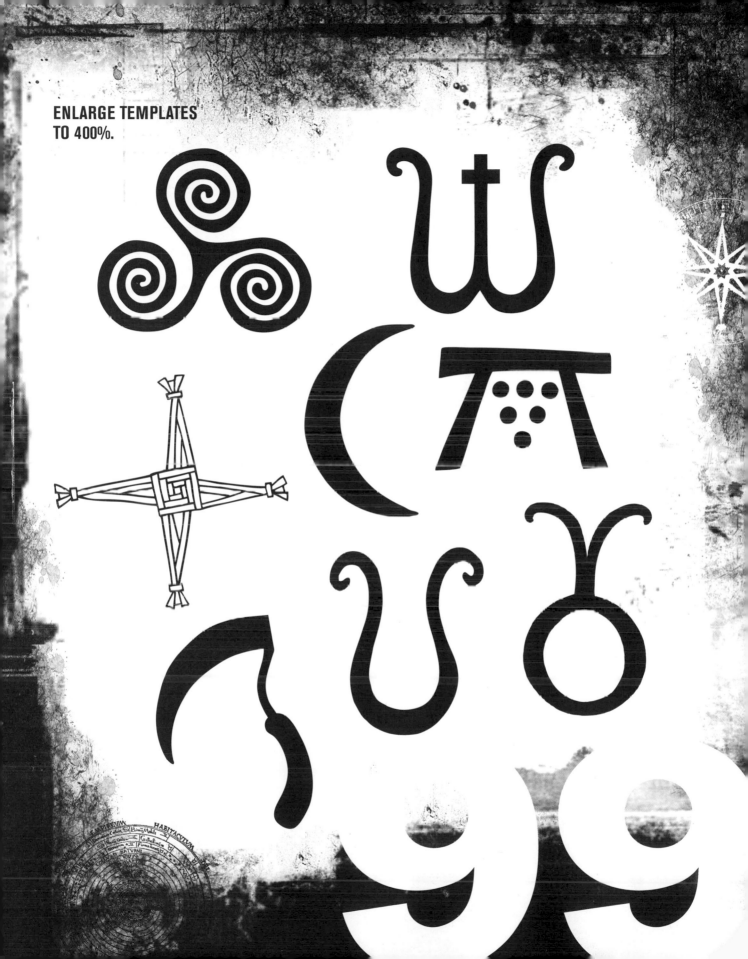

ENLARGE TEMPLATES
TO 400%.

Twelve days of Christmas, eight days of Chanukah, seven days of Kwanzaa, two nasturtiums, and a partridge in a pear tree. That's right, we're going to talk holidays, Pagan style, but you needn't cringe in fear. There will be no mass consumerism, no keeping up with the Jonses' decorations, and absolutely no guilt trip from your family, 'cause we honestly don't care if you never write or you never call. (What's with that anyway? Does your hand cramp up when it gets near a phone? You could at least e-mail. We worry, you know. We worry because we love you.)

WE'RE ALL UNIQUE IN
EXACTLY THE SAME WAY

Paganism, like Christianity, Judaism, and Islam, has many different flavors and denominations. It may actually have more than the Big Three combined, as the term Paganism encompasses any non-Abrahamic religion, which would include the Hindus if they felt inclined to accept the label. (That inclination, the authors must guess, would vary wildly from individual to individual, as humans are capricious beasts at best.) Because of this variation, it is difficult to present any information labeled as "Pagan" without pissing someone off for being left out. What follows, then, is a description of the Pagan calendar as Zabet celebrates it in her own personal flavor of Paganism, which one might call Irish Greco-Persian Eclecticism. Most Western Pagans reading this will find it quite familiar, but perhaps not exactly like their own.

WHICH WITCH IS WHICH?

Probably the most well known of the modern Western Pagan religions is Wicca, which began in the mid-twentieth century and was devised by British occultist Gerald Gardner. (For more information on the process of turning fragments of knowledge into a full-blown religion with rules, read "Wiccan Revival," chapter 4 of *Drawing Down the Moon* by Margot Adler.) Wicca is the closest thing to an organized religion that there is in modern Western Paganism, and even then there are several Wiccan splinter groups. Wiccans often refer to themselves as Witches, though there are others who use the term Witch and mean a family tradition of witchcraft, uninfluenced by Gerald Gardner in any way, and are not practitioners of Wicca. Zabet does not claim to be either kind of Witch; she is simply Pagan. Because of Wicca's popularity and organization, many modern non-Wiccan Pagans still borrow from Wiccan vocabulary and imagery, as a sort of *lingua franca* to make communication between Pagans easier.

BIG WHEEL KEEP ON TURNIN'

There are eight main holidays divided neatly between the twelve months of the year. As Pagans tend to see the cyclical nature of things, we like to represent the calendar as a circle instead of a row of boxes. Thinking of that circle, at the 12 o'clock, 3 o'clock, 6 o'clock, and 9 o'clock positions are the Quarter holidays. Their names are, respectively, Yule (Winter Solstice), Ostara (Spring Equinox), Litha (Summer Solstice), and Mabon (Fall Equinox). For those of you who were too busy throwing spitballs during astronomy class in school, an equinox occurs when the Earth is at a certain position in its orbit around the Sun, midway between when it is closest to the sun and when it is farthest. On an equinox day, the length of the day and night are equal. Equinoxes occur twice a year in the spring and fall. A solstice, on the other hand, happens when the Earth is either as far away from the Sun as it can get, or as close as it can get, and the difference in the length of day and night are at their most dramatic. At Winter Solstice, we see the longest night of the year; Summer Solstice marks the longest day.

Ancient Pagans proved to be quite crafty in figuring out the dates these astronomical events occurred. For example, the Newgrange mound in Britain built in 3200 B.C.E. has a single-entrance passageway that is lit by sunlight only at sunrise on Winter Solstice. Modern Pagans have it much easier; Zabet is fond of the U.S. Naval Observatory website, which will give you not only the date, but the exact time of every equinox and solstice for a hundred years. What can we say? Zabet is a geek.

The remaining four holidays are called Cross-Quarter holidays, as they sit on the midpoints between the Quarter holidays. They are Imbolc, Beltane, Lughnadsah, and Samhain. Fans of *The AntiCraft* online zine should recognize those names because we use them to denote our issues rather than saying "Spring, Summer, Fall, Winter." Yes, we did it to be snobbish and difficult, and we're proud of it.

I CAME, I SAW, I INVENTED MY OWN CALENDAR

To muddle things further, some Pagans like to ignore the twelve-day calendar shift that occurred as the modern world switched from the Julian calendar to the Gregorian calendar (a process beginning in 1582 and spanning three and a half centuries to get everyone's ducks in the same row). Therefore, the dates that follow may or may not be changed by up to twelve days.

I COME FROM THE LAND DOWN UNDER

But wait, there's more! As the holidays are linked to the seasons, Pagans living in the southern hemisphere will have a completely reversed calendar. December and Christmas might fall in the middle of summer, but Yule will not be celebrated until it's actually winter —in June!

MOUSEKETEER ROLL CALL

Each holiday celebrates what is going on in the world around us at that particular time of the year. Zabet lives in the northern hemisphere—hence, holidays are listed as such. See the illustration of the Southern Hemisphere Wheel of the Year (page 103) to help you figure out what's going on Down Under. The descriptions will still apply; it's only the time of year you celebrate that changes.

YULE—WINTER SOLSTICE (DECEMBER 22 OR THEREABOUTS)

This is the start of the year. It is the shortest day, and therefore every day thereafter is longer and longer. Think of the year waxing and waning like the moon. This is when the year begins to progress toward its fullest, most bountiful point.

IMBOLC—FEBRUARY 1

Traditionally a time for lambs and calves to be born in Britain, this holiday centers around spring fertility and dairy products. At Zabet's house, flaming cheese is a favorite dish.

OSTARA—SPRING EQUINOX (MARCH 22 OR THEREABOUTS)

This Germanic word is related to our modern word "Easter." It is commonly accepted that the word Ostara is the name of a goddess of fertility, related to the Anglo-Saxon goddess Eostre, and what better symbols of that than the ever-fornicating rabbit and all those lovely eggs?

BELTANE—MAY 1

Also called May Day, this holiday has lots to do with fire, sunlight, and sex. It's gettin' it on time if you (or your animals) haven't gotten it on yet. The crops are budding in the fields and the sun is nourishing them.

LITHA—SUMMER SOLSTICE (JUNE 22 OR THEREABOUTS)

This is the longest day of the year. Going back to our "waxing and waning" metaphor, this is when the year is full. Everything is full of light and warmth, and it's only going to go downhill from here on out.

LUGHNASADH—AUGUST 1

This is the harvest holiday. Wheat, corn, squash, and other veggies are being brought in. Canning and preparing for the winter is in full swing. The promise of fall is in the air, and ye olde agricultural societies would be working their butts off, racing against the clock for the coming winter.

MABON—FALL EQUINOX (SEPTEMBER 22 OR THEREABOUTS)

The year is begining to wane. Leaves are changing; things are slowing down for the winter. Plants are dying off. Days will become noticeably shorter afterward.

SAMHAIN—NOVEMBER 1

From the Gaelic for "Summer's End," this holiday welcomes in winter. It's an odd time of year, when we are still carried by the bounty of the harvest but things have not yet entirely died out. Many believe the veil between the world of the living and the world of the dead is thinner at this time. It's good for turning inward and contemplating your life and what you want to do with it. It's a quietening of the world, a liminal point between years, a little death, time to recuperate.

DUDE, THAT'S JUST CRAZY

In conclusion, all this crap is part of why Renée thinks religion is a mental illness. Zabet is too busy talking to trees to argue with her.

SOURCES:

Am I a Hindu? The Hinduism Primer
by Ed. Viswanathan
Drawing Down the Moon by Margot Adler
A Guide to Britain's Pagan Heritage by David Clarke
Hekate in Ancient Greek Religion by Robert Von Rudloff
Newgrange: Archeology, Art and Legend by Michael J. O'Kelly
The Rosemoon Guild, conversations with members both at and outside of official Guild meetings, 1994-2003
Who's Who in Non-Classical Mythology by Egerton Sykes

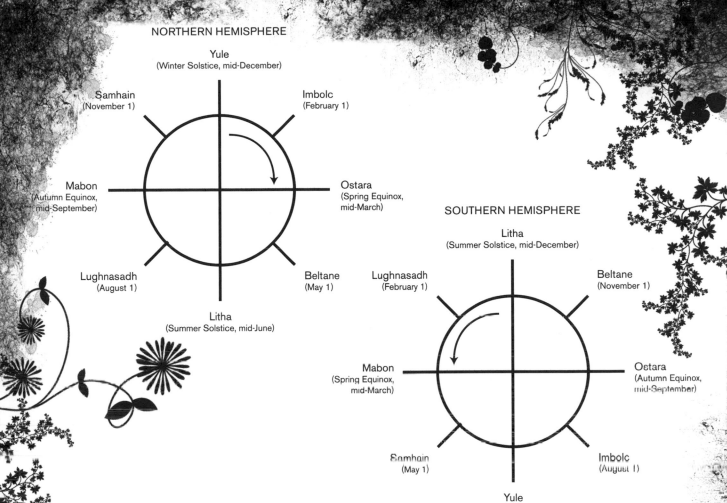

NORTHERN HEMISPHERE

Yule
(Winter Solstice, mid-December)

Samhain
(November 1)

Imbolc
(February 1)

Mabon
(Autumn Equinox,
mid-September)

Ostara
(Spring Equinox,
mid-March)

Lughnasadh
(August 1)

Beltane
(May 1)

Litha
(Summer Solstice, mid-June)

SOUTHERN HEMISPHERE

Litha
(Summer Solstice, mid-December)

Lughnasadh
(February 1)

Beltane
(November 1)

Mabon
(Spring Equinox,
mid-March)

Ostara
(Autumn Equinox,
mid-September)

Samhain
(May 1)

Imbolc
(August 1)

Yule
(Winter Solstice, mid-June)

Holiday	Panel Color (Piece C)	Appliqué Color	Appliqué Thread	Symbol and Meaning	
Samhain	Black	Rust Orange		The triskele is a symbol with many meanings, used here at the New Year to mean rebirth and reincarnation.	
Yule	Green	Red	White	Winter	
Imbolc	Pale Yellow	White	Silver	St. Bridgit's Cross is associated with fertility. Her festival coincides with Imbolc.	
Ostara	Pale Green	Yellow	Light Orange	Spring	
Beltane	White	Red	Silver	The waxing moon signifies the increasing light and approaching summer.	
Litha	Bright Yellow	Green	Light Green	Summer	
Lunghnasadh	Rust Orange	Dark Brown	Green	The sickle is a symbol of the harvest. The blade also resembles the shape of the waning moon.	
Mabon	Maroon	Light Brown	Yellow Ochre	Fall	

Alex Trebek was actually born Quator Theornak from the planet of Canada. After a decadent childhood filled with eight Pop-Tarts to a box and more Cadbury than you could shake a stick at—no literally, we tried—he chose a life of asceticism and moved to Los Angeles to further his quest for the perfect answer in the form of a question. Using his mad alien skillz, he mind melded with television executives, forcing a decision to give him an internationally popular game show. It wasn't called *Jeopardy* for nothing, as those executives lost their lives because their feeble minds could not handle the awesome brainpower of the extra-terrestrial. We say that to say this: We couldn't call this section "Potpourri" because *Jeopardy* might sue us. Instead, we invented the world miscellany. We hope you enjoy its caramely *mmm-mm* beginning, its smooth dark chocolate *eeeeeee* finish, and its slightly hissy nougat center.

FOREVER BOUND

BY LAELIA WADE

Here is a fine garment made from one of the handiest materials on earth—duct tape! Not only can you hold your ducts together, but you can look fairly stylish doing it. This project is designed to fit your size and dimensions exactly, which will also help prevent others from stealing it from your wardrobe. And even a somewhat half-assed attempt can yield some pretty awesome results!

Duct tape fashions are fairly popular with some fashionistas (some go as far as to craft gowns and suits from the wonderful material), although it can be difficult to find instructions for how to actually make the garments. Your intrepid duct tape seamstress is then left with little recourse other then a few amazing pictures and her own imagination. A quick search on the Internet can come up with all sorts of entries that may or may not help, but are pretty interesting anyway—and new things appear every day!

MATERIALS AND TOOLS:

1 roll extra-sturdy duct tape
1 roll black duct tape, or color of your choice
Sturdy scissors that can cut through several layers of duct tape and a T-shirt
Grommets
Grommet tool
Hammer
Hard surface (such as a concrete floor)
Your choice of lacing (long shoelaces, ribbon, thin rope, string)
T-shirt that can be cut up and, for all intents and purposes, destroyed

MOOD ENHANCERS:

There are several ways to get into the proper mood for this project, but that would partly depend on the final intentions. For instance, if you were making it for a pirate or wench-type costume you might prefer to sing sea shanties and watch pirate or Victorian-era style movies. If you want to wear this to a rave or for futuristic outfits, I might recommend listening to some German techno-industrial music. Although beverages such as rum could be useful in getting you "in the mood" for the project, I would advise against it until well past the stages where you could easily inflict personal harm.

SKILLS USED:

Ability to make friends and bend them to your will

1. Put on the T-shirt with a minimum of undergarments; you don't want to accidentally cut up your best bra or favorite jeans. If it's not already snug, try to pull all of the excess material toward where the opening of your corset will be (in this case, the front).

2. Have a friend you trust (or yourself, in front of a full-length mirror), take long lengths of the duct tape and begin wrapping them around your torso, over the T-shirt. Start at the top and work your way down. Overlap each piece to ensure structural integrity. You want the duct tape to be snug, while still being able to breathe and not feel as though you're going to pass out. Complete the first layer in the general shape you want the corset to be.

3. Begin a second, final layer of tape, using the color of your choice. Start at the top and adhere the tape like you did for the first layer, covering the foundation layer. Make sure you overlap the tape as you go.

4. By now, breathing may be difficult and you will most likely feel hot. Fear not—the end of the torture is near. Take the scissors and cut a straight line down (or up) where you want the final opening to be. In this case, it is the front, as I want to be able to close it myself. Take it slowly and patiently.

5. Now that you can remove the corset, cut away the excess T-shirt. You can leave the portion of the shirt that's stuck to the tape as-is to act as a sort of lining. Make sure you can recognize which way is "up" on the corset.

6. Carefully cover the raw edges of the corset with duct tape by folding pieces in half, centered over the edge. Due to the curve of the finished piece, you may need to use small pieces and overlap them. Reinforce the edges where you cut the corset open with additional duct tape, as this portion will endure the most stress while wearing the garment.

7. Attach the grommets along the cut-open edges, according to the package instructions. Take some time to measure so they will be evenly spaced and there are the same number of grommet holes on each side. Lace up and you're good-to-go!

Hallowed Counsel

The OCD crafter says: Duct tape is not for OCD crafters. There will always be imperfections, no matter how you cut or measure it. Love the flaws.

—Shannon Mock

Designer bio:

I am from the Great White North, more specifically, Vancouver, Canada. Due to the wet, cold, dark, and otherwise boring winters here, crafting is a significant part of life, especially if you do not have cable TV and cannot play guitar. I have been a part of a craft group for several years now, and it was through this that I came to know of *The AntiCraft* and rejoiced in finding others who appreciate crafts that do not involve fuzzy, pink yarn toques.

I knit, crochet, and have a fondness for glue and duct tape. I am also fond of fire, but when I involve that with crafts the results are often disastrous. The same goes for alcohol—never drink and decoupage! I am also an artist with a bachelor's degree in fine arts and anthropology. My artwork can be viewed online at www .laeliawade.com for those who may be interested.

I would like to thank Jenn for showing me the site, Sheryl for correcting my spelling and punctuation, and friends and family for either encouraging me or making fun of me. You know who you are and what you did.

@#$%!! *%^*≤@@#!
!@#$%^ $$@!

かわいい！

OH COME ON!

HELL NO!

CHANDELIERS

BY ROBYN ROSEN

These earrings are a unique interpretation of the ever-popular "chandelier" style earrings. Based on the European 4-1 chainmail weave, most commonly seen in Medieval armor, the rosette pattern adds a romantic and feminine touch, giving the earrings a flowery appearance. Black jump rings make these earrings darkly beautiful, while the shimmering fire-polished glass beads and dainty pewter bats add playful accents.

This project is great for the beginning chainmail weaver, with step-by-step instructions on how to properly open and close jump rings and construct the European chainmail weave. Once you have mastered the techniques shown, you will be able to make yourself a variety of complimentary chainmail pieces, such as bracelets, necklaces, and even simple headpieces.

MOOD ENHANCERS:

Chicks 'N Chained Males edited by Esther Friesner

SKILLS USED:

Basic beading
Basic chainmail (as explained in project instructions)
European 4-1 (see page 154)

MATERIALS AND TOOLS:

10 top-drilled Vitrial teardrop fire-polished glass beads
2 pewter bat charms
10" (25cm) 20-gauge black enameled copper wire
24 18-gauge, ³⁄₁₆" ID black anodized aluminum jump rings
2 pairs chain-nosed pliers
Round-nose pliers
Flush wire cutters

NOTES:

Smooth and even closures are the foundation for a professional-quality piece of chainmail. I encourage you to spend some time practicing opening and closing jump rings before you move on to constructing your earrings to ensure that you make a flawless piece of jewelry for yourself. To begin this project, practice the steps for chainmail on pages 154–155.

Make the rosettes:

1. Open twelve jump rings and close another twelve jump rings to get yourself set up.
2. Place 4 closed rings on 1 open ring and close.
3. Lay flat with two closed rings on either side of the ring you closed in Step 2. Note how this is the seed of the European 4 in 1 pattern. All of the rings on the left and right side of this project will need to face the same direction for this pattern to be even.
4. If you need to, flip the piece onto the other side or rotate it so the part of the middle ring that lays over the side rings is at the bottom and the part that lays under the side rings is at the top. The side rings will be laying the opposite direction of the middle ring.
5. Pass an open ring through the top 2 rings in the chain in such a way that mimics the middle ring—the part that lays over the other rings should be at the bottom—but do not close this ring yet.
6. Add one closed jump ring to either side of the open jump ring and close. (You may wish to lay the piece flat again to make sure the rings are still facing the same direction.)

7. Pass one open jump ring through the last pair of closed jump rings added (you are adding another middle ring, as in Step 5), add an earring hook onto this ring, and close. Make sure the earring hook front is on the same side of the chainmail as should be facing up when you lay the chainmail on the table.

8. Pass one open jump ring through the bottommost pair of side rings and close. (You are adding another middle ring as in Step 5.)

9. Lay the piece flat on your work surface. Take one open jump ring and pass through the 3 rings on one side of the chainmail piece and close. Repeat this step on the opposite side of the piece and you will have one rosette chainmail segment that will become the base of your chandelier earring. Both of these rings should lay in the same direction as the middle ring even though they go through three side rings instead of just two.

Beaded eyepin:

1. Cut a ¾" (2cm) piece of the black enameled copper wire. Bend the wire at a right angle, leaving a tail of just over ¼" (6mm).

2. Grasp wire just above the bend with the round-nose pliers. Wrap wire around nose of pliers to form loop.

3. Place one of the teardrop beads (wider end pointing down) onto the wire and bend the wire at a right angle just above the bead, using chain-nose pliers.

4. Trim the tail to just over ¼" (6mm), grasp wire just above the bend with round-nose pliers, and wrap the wire around the nose of the pliers to form a loop.

5. Open the loop closest to the narrow end of the bead by grasping the cut end of the loop with chain-nose pliers and bending open just far enough to slip the loop over the jump ring at the bottom center of your chainmail earring. Attach a beaded eyepin to the earring and close.

6. Open the loop on the opposite end of the eyepin, slip the bat charm onto the wire and close.

Beaded headpins:

1. Cut four ¾" (2cm) pieces of black enameled copper wire.

2. Grasp the wire with the chain-nose pliers leaving a ¹⁄₁₆" (2mm) tail and bend toward the body of the wire as far as you can go. There will be a small loop. Grasp this loop with the tips of the chain-nose pliers and press flat to create the head of the pin.

3. Place one teardrop bead onto the headpin with the wide end on the bottom. Bend the wire at a right angle just above the bead using chain-nose pliers.

4. Trim the tail to just over ¼" (6mm), grasp the wire just above the bend with round-nose pliers, and wrap the wire around the nose of the pliers to form a loop.

5. Open the loop by grasping the cut end of the loop with chain-nose pliers and bending open just far enough to slip the loop over one of the jump rings.

Repeat steps 2–5 for the rest of the wire segments and attach to the jump rings on the bottom sections of the earrings.

Unless you've run out of holes in your head, you'll need two. Repeat to create a matching earring.

Designer bio:

Robyn Rosen has been creating unique chainmail, wirework, and beaded jewelry for more than ten years and has recently begun teaching chainmail classes locally in central New Jersey. She has had her chainmail jewelry projects published in magazines such as *Step-by-Step Wire* and *Bead Style*. She also sells complete DIY Chainmail making kits in her Etsy shop at www.robynrosen.etsy.com and on her homepage at www.robynrosen.com. She also has a certificate in graphic design and is currently a student in computer science, in an effort to become a well-rounded artsy-crafty geek, with a little bit of computer geek thrown in for good measure.

MIDNIGHT STAR

BY ANDREA L. STERN

The full moon rises on a crystal cold night. Ice-covered branches glisten beneath the glow. In the castle, a sole light is lit, casting its warm glow onto the snow below. A highwayman awaits on his dark horse, waiting for the maiden to come to him, dressed in her finest velvet cloak, this necklace adorning her pale throat.

MOOD ENHANCERS:

"The Highwayman," *The Book of Secrets*
by Loreena McKennitt

SKILLS USED:

Basic beading
Circular flat peyote (see page 153)

MATERIALS AND TOOLS:

1 30mm button with shank
25g 11/0 seed beads
38 5mm x 8mm curved petal or leaf beads
93 3mm round beads
65 4mm bicone crystal beads
Clasp and spring ring
#12 beading needles
Thread
Wax
Scissors

Hallowed Counsel

A good way to keep your beads from going everywhere is to work inside a silicone baking pan. If you drop a bead, it will not bounce out and your dropped beads will stay corralled.

—Renée

1. Thread the needle, pulling ends to meet each other and knot. Sew through the shank of the button, wrapping around in a figure eight and sewing through the thread to secure.
2. String twenty-one beads and sew through the first bead to make a circle, encircling the shank. Add or reduce beads as necessary to fit shank.
3. Peyote stitch one round.
4. Next round, increase every other space by picking up two beads instead of one.
5. Peyote stitch one round, adding a bead in between the two beads of each increase.
6. Peyote stitch one round.
Repeat Steps 3–6 three times, or until the beadwork reaches the edge of the button. End with adding a bead in between the two beads of each increase—this creates a picot-like bump around the edge of the button.
7. Weave the needle through the beads so it comes out the first bead of increase picot.
8. String a 3mm round, a crystal bead and a 3mm round. Sew through the next picot. Repeat until one space remains, save that for the fringe.
9. Sew through the last picot and string the following beads for the fringes: five 11/0 seed beads, a 3mm round, a crystal bead, a 3mm round, three 11/0 seed beads, a petal bead, a crystal bead, a petal bead, a crystal bead, a petal bead, three 11/0 seed beads, a 3mm round, a crystal bead, a 3mm round and five 11/0 seed beads. Sew back through the picot on the other side of the gap.

Designer bio:

Andrea L. Stern has been making art her whole life, and playing with beads for over sixteen years. Her work encompasses a wide range of media, from art quilts, to beadwork, plush animals, and embroideries, and has been exhibited nationally and internationally. Her favorite day would include working in her studio with her sons and hanging at the local coffeeshop with her daughters, ending with a nice meal of homemade pizza with the whole family.

10. Weave through to the bead next to the picot and string the following beads for the next fringe: (two 11/0 seed beads, a 3mm round)×9, two 11/0 seed beads. Sew back through the corresponding bead on the opposite side.

11. Weave through the inside bead and string the following beads for the next fringe: three 11/0 seed beads, a crystal bead, five 11/0 seed beads, a petal bead, five 11/0 seed beads, a crystal bead, and three 11/0 seed beads. Weave ends in. An additional fringe can be added in the center if there is a gap or if additional fullness is desired.

12. There are now two beads between the beginning and end of each picot. Weave back to one side and string the following to create a framing fringe for the picots: three 11/0 seed beads, a 3mm round, three 11/0 seed beads. Sew back into the corresponding bead on the other side of the gap.

13. With a new thread and needle, weave through the backing beads and come out on one side (there should be two picots at the top of the pendant, the stranded beads come out from each side of those two picots).

14. String the following pattern: (five 11/0 seed beads, a 3mm round, a crystal bead, a 3mm round, five 11/0 seed beads, and a petal bead)×5, (five 11/0 seed beads, a 3mm round, a crystal bead, and a 3mm round)×3, and five 11/0 seed beads. Add the clasp or spring ring, sewing back through the threaded beads and coming back out at the fourth crystal from the clasp.

15. String the following beads for the drop fringe: three 11/0 seed beads, a 3mm round, a crystal bead, a petal bead, a crystal bead, a petal bead, a crystal bead, a petal bead, a crystal bead, a 3mm round, and three 11/0 seed beads. Sew through the crystal in the next pattern four times.

16. Weave through the beads on the back.

A BLACKBIRD'S SECRET

BY RACHEL YOUNG

Blackbirds are said to be guardians of all the great secrets of the universe. This small, elegant case can hold a few secrets of your own.

The case has an embossed metal outer layer, a chip board core, and a felt lining. The lid is a fitted cap, containing a small mirror, which can move on and off the tube by sliding along the ribbon or chain attached to the tube. The long chain and flashy tassel evoke a 1920s-style necklace, but the case can also be fitted with shorter ribbon, which can tie in a bow to secure the lid onto the case.

My first inspiration for this project was to create a fancy vessel for a square of ink-jet silk, printed with my local bus map, but any image will do. Simply print on Jacquard ink-jet silk, peel from the paper, hem the edges, and stuff it into your new case. Then it can be produced, magician-style, at any opportune moment. I like to add a charm, bead, or small tassel (hooray for tassels!) to the corner of the silk for easy removal from the case.

I suggest the following cargo: Lipstick; perfume; a lock of hair; a single tampon; or silk, printed with:

- Maps: treasure, local bus, hometown, or favorite place.
- Useful information: a Latin conjugation chart, the periodic table of the elements, or a star chart.
- Pictures: friends, family or those quirky ancestors who wore doilies on their heads.
- Your favorite poem or image.
- The words to the spell you're casting later.
- Grandma's Secret Gingerbread Recipe.

MOOD ENHANCERS:

Thirteen Ways of Looking at a Blackbird
by Wallace Stevens

SKILLS USED:

Embossing (as explained in project instructions)
Extreme patience
A gentle love of accuracy

Hallowed Counsel

Always use a glue appropriate to the materials being glued. When in doubt, check out www.thistothat.com, where you can choose the materials and it will automatically recommend glues for you.

—Rachel Young

15

MATERIALS AND TOOLS:

Aluminum embossing metal

$\frac{1}{32}$" (1mm) thick chipboard (brown cardboard, usually found supporting packages of finer paper—a cereal box would work as well)

$\frac{1}{16}$" (2mm) thick mat board

28-gauge craft wire (sliver or black color)

12" × 12" (30cm × 30cm) $\frac{1}{16}$" (2mm) thick steel gray wool felt

$\frac{3}{4}$" (2cm) diameter shisha mirror

19-gauge dark annealed wire (bent into a jump ring with an inner diameter of $\frac{9}{16}$" [14mm])

Small beads for tassel

Tassel top (or "cap": a hollow, bell-shaped finding used on the ends of multi-stranded necklaces)

Soldered jump ring (must fit comfortably inside tassel top and have no seam)

Seamed jump rings (2 in small gauge to match chain)

Swarovski crystals or other beads (for tassel and chain decoration)

36" (91cm) thin chain or ribbon

Fine-grit sandpaper

Folded newspaper

Thin masking or framing tape

Ballpoint pen (for embossing the metal)

Blunt embossing tool, such as a pointy chopstick or clay tools

Soft wax, such as beeswax or cheesewax

Sharp scissors capable of cutting metal

Needle or needle tool

Shiny black nail polish

Nail polish remover

Cotton swabs or cloth for removing nail polish

Weldbond Universal Adhesive (a rockin' white glue for non-metal gluing)

Round toothpicks or de-cottoned cotton swabs (for molding metal and wire around)

UHU Creative 2-part metal glue or JB Weld (for metal only)

Rubber bands

Fitted rubber gloves for use with metal glue

Wine cork

Needle-nose pliers

Flat-nose pliers

Round-nose pliers (optional)

Tweezers or a dexterous child

Bead thread

Bead needle

Craft knife

Cutting mat

Embossing:

Testing these tools and techniques on a scrap is highly recommended. Forcing the metal too quickly or too far can lead to unsightly holes and cracks, so keep this in mind while embossing and assembling the pieces. Work fine lines from the front with a ball point pen and from the back with a slightly duller tool, whenever possible. In some cases, the pen will be the only tool small enough to work fine details, but use your best judgment. Work open areas with a larger, rounder tool, such as a popsicle stick.

1. Lightly sand both sides of the sheet of foil and wipe away dust with a cloth. This will keep the polish from chipping later.

2. Tape a copy of the template (page 120) pieces to the foil and place on a thin pad of folded newspaper. Trace over the lines to transfer. Remove template. You may want to separate the pieces for easier embossing. Cut them out generally, avoiding their actual outlines.

3. To best explain the relief levels of this piece, a topography map of the tube skin is included for reference (page 120). Think of the un-embossed metal as sea level. From the front, with a slightly thicker pad of paper underneath, go over traced lines and add any remaining "below sea level" lines for all pieces. For the tube skin background, any kind of small, close pattern will do if curlicues make you crazy. Traditional origami paper is a good source for such patterns.

4. When your lines and shapes have been worked into nice little ditches, work the negative areas from the back with no pad underneath. Set the smaller pieces aside.

5. Replace the pad and slowly work the plants and bird from the back to desired degree of relief. Work details into the bird from the back with the pen.

6. Warm small pieces of wax in your hands and fill the backs of the plant and bird shapes to lend structural support. The wax should be flush with sea level, or just shy of it.

7. Work details, if desired, into the plants from the front. Check that the wax is still flush with the back surface and remove any that sticks out.

8. Cut out your pieces. Remember to make interior cuts as well. Punch the hole in the tube base cover with a needle or needle tool, but only mark the four holes in the tube skin. They will be punched later.

Polish:

1. Paint background areas with nail polish and let them dry for several hours. (Try to fill the fine lines, avoid polishing above the filigree line on the tube skin. This will only be covered by the lid.)

2. Remove surface polish with a cotton swab or cloth dipped in nail polish remover. The fine lines should now be the only

thing filled with polish. No polish is needed in the indented tab areas on both sides of the tube skin. These will be covered by the tabs on the opposite edge.

3. Repeat this process with the plants and bird. Also, paint the back of the mirror frame and set it aside.

Tube skeleton:

1. For the main tube, cut a 3" × 3 " (8cm × 8cm) rectangle from the chipboard with the longer edges parallel with the grain. This makes the cardboard easier to form into a tube. Mark a ¼" (6mm) wide stripe along one of the longer edges.

2. For the side of the lid, cut a ½" × 3½" (13mm × 9cm) rectangle from the chipboard with the short edge parallel to the grain. Mark a ¼" (6mm) wide stripe along one of the longer edges.

3. Using the template, cut out the lid top pattern and tube base pattern, complete with two punched holes, from the mat board.

4. Slightly sand the sharp edges from the mat board circles.

5. Curl the two pieces of chipboard over the edge of a table or around a ruler, like curling ribbon, or roll them gently around a pencil to get them to curve. Glue each piece into a tube, overlapping on ¼" (6mm) strips indicated. Let dry. Sand along the outside seams to reduce the sharp, stair-step edge created by the overlap.

6. Feed each end of a 6" (15cm) length of beading wire through one of the two holes in the bottom mat board circle, as though it were a button. Twist the ends together once or twice against the mat board to secure.

7. Glue a scrap of felt to the side of the circle where the wire does not emerge. When dry, trim the felt to the size of the circle.

8. Center the shisha mirror on one side of the mat board lid circle and glue in place.

9. Tape the tube base circle onto the end of the tube. Use one layer only of thin masking or framing tape. The circle should not fit inside the tube, but be flush with the end. The felt should face the inside of the tube, with the wire pointing out.

10. Place the large jump ring over the wrong side of the mirror frame. Push the center bits through the ring and fold them outward as far as they will go, hugging the ring to the frame.

11. Center the mirror frame, wrong side against the mirror, and tightly wrap the metal edges around the mat board circle, conforming to its shape as closely as possible.

12. Tape the mirror frame assembly to the small chipboard loop, as in step 9. The mirror side faces inside the lid, while the messy side shows as the top of the lid.

13. Fold the centers of the chain holders over a round toothpick, stripped cotton swab, or other object slightly larger than the chain you are using, and insert the ends into the pairs of slots in the lid skin metal. Fold the ends of each chain

holder away from each other crisply, so they lie against the back of the lid skin.

14. Reinforce the fold lines on the lid skin and tube base cover by tracing over them from the back with the pen. Gently curve the tube skin and lid skin metal pieces to conform to their chipboard counterparts. It's OK if they are a bit springy.

Bust out the 2-part metal glue:

Read all cautions on product! As a rule: good ventilation and gloves are a must. Practice application on those tooling scraps you were playing with earlier until you are comfortable. Rubber bands can be used to keep the pieces in place while they dry, just make sure you don't glue them on!

If you can avoid gluing ¼" (6mm) from the open end of both the tube skin and the lid skin, this will help you later on (see Lining, Step 1).

1. Glue on the lid top, centering over the messy side of the mat board circle.

2. For the lid skin, glue the ends of the chain holder strips to the back. Tuck the rectangular tab under the opposite edge to make a straight seam. Glue in place or slide onto chipboard after gluing, then fold the petals toward the center of the top circle, placing them at intervals that match the filigree, and adhere in place.

3. For the tube skin, glue the five triangular tabs on each long edge, adhering them to their corresponding indentations on the opposite edge. The two rectangular tabs tuck underneath the opposite edges, giving a straight vertical seam at the top and bottom. Slide the tube skin onto the chipboard tube so the bottom edge of metal is flush with the bottom of the tube base.

4. For the tube base cover, thread the wire through the hole in the center and slide the cover into place. Fold the petals up and glue to the tube side with one of the larger petals centered over the vertical seam.

5. Put that glue away! Let everything dry.

Hardware:

1. Place a cork into the mouth of the tube, far enough to sit under the hole punch marks in the tube skin. Punch these holes through the metal and the chipboard with a needle tool, using the cork as a support.

2. For each set of holes, thread each end of a 4"–5" (10cm–13cm) length of beading wire through one of the two holes from the inside to the outside. Wrap each wire over a toothpick or similar object held against the tube, and take each end back into the opposite hole. Twist the ends together to secure against the inside wall, cut the excess wire, and cover the holes and wire with a piece of tape (tweezers, needle-nose pliers, or a dexterous child are handy tools for this step).

Lining:

1. Cut a 3⅛" × 2⁹⁄₁₆" (8cm × 7cm) rectangle and a 3⅛" × ⅜" (8cm x 1cm) rectangle from the felt.

2. Roll the larger piece of felt tightly enough to slip inside the tube. Use your fingers to unroll and ease the felt into place. The edges should butt up against each other and not overlap.

3. Place the small rectangle inside the lid. Use a very small amount of glue to secure this piece. There is no need to glue the larger piece, but you may.

4. The excess metal for both the tube and the lid must now be turned in. Fold the metal over the top of the chipboard and the felt. This is asking a lot of the metal, so do not attempt this from all sides at once! Start with the innermost corner of overlapped metal and work your way around, using your thumb to fold the metal over and in. There will be wrinkles because the metal is being forced to occupy a smaller space. To finish, use pliers over a protective scrap of felt to make a crisp edge and flatten the wrinkles.

Tassel chain:

1. Make one tassel strand by stringing 1½" (4cm) of small beads, then go back through all but the last one, which will act as a stopper. Don't pull the thread too tight or the tassel will stick out in every direction. Go through the soldered jump ring and repeat until you have a number of strands on both sides of the jump ring (like a limp bow tie).

2. Experiment to see how many strands fit comfortably inside the tassel top. Tie the ends together, draw the threads through the beads on one of the tassel strands and trim off the excess thread.

3. Run the beading wire through the jump ring and fold in half. Run both ends up through the tassel top and a larger bead. Pull snug, and loop both ends around pliers or a round toothpick and wrap them around themselves a few times. Trim neatly. Now you have a tassel with a metal loop on top.

4. Run wires from the tube base through the tassel loop and wrap them back around themselves as in step 3.

5. Add Swarovski crystals or other beads to the chain by cutting the chain and hooking in beads threaded on wire. Do not add beads closer than 4" (10cm) to both ends of the chain.

6. Thread each end of the chain through one of the chain holders in the lid and secure to the loops on the sides of the tube with jump rings. Make sure the vertical seams on the lid and tube are facing the same direction.

7. Do a little dance of satisfaction.

Metal Embossing Templates

(All pattern pieces are for metal except where noted)

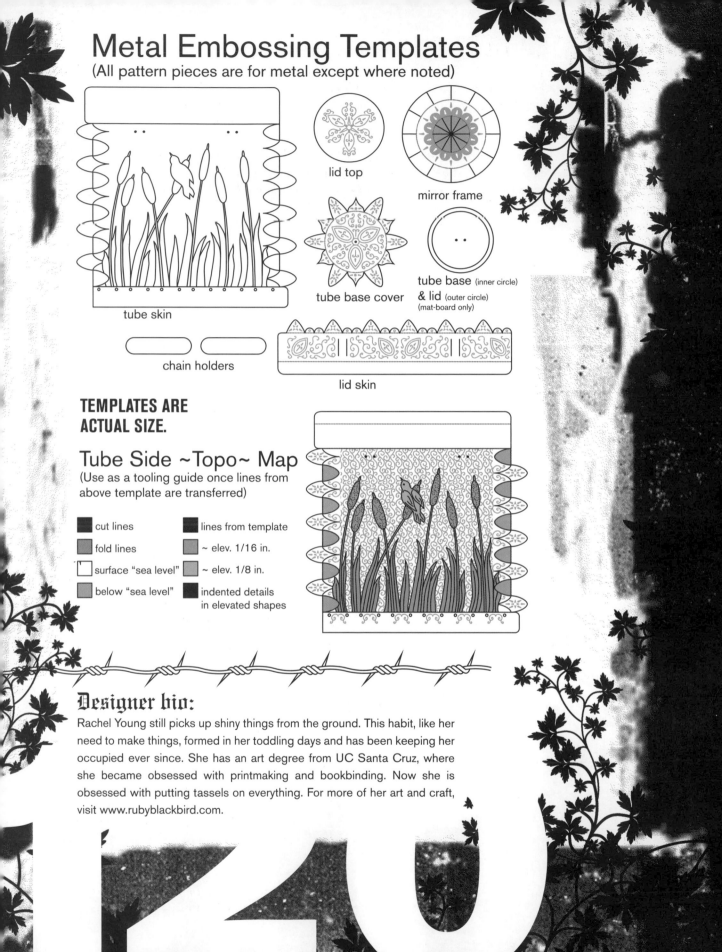

tube skin

lid top

mirror frame

tube base cover

tube base (inner circle)
& lid (outer circle)
(mat-board only)

chain holders

lid skin

TEMPLATES ARE ACTUAL SIZE.

Tube Side ~Topo~ Map
(Use as a tooling guide once lines from above template are transferred)

- cut lines
- fold lines
- surface "sea level"
- below "sea level"
- lines from template
- ~ elev. 1/16 in.
- ~ elev. 1/8 in.
- indented details in elevated shapes

Designer bio:

Rachel Young still picks up shiny things from the ground. This habit, like her need to make things, formed in her toddling days and has been keeping her occupied ever since. She has an art degree from UC Santa Cruz, where she became obsessed with printmaking and bookbinding. Now she is obsessed with putting tassels on everything. For more of her art and craft, visit www.rubyblackbird.com.

CRAFT-RELATED INJURIES by Heather Hard, M.D.

First of all, a general disclaimer: If you think you need to see a doctor about an injury, you probably do. When using pointy, sharp things, or things that burn stuff, try to not only avoid distractions, but to keep things clean. Now I'm not talking the PG kind of clean, I'm talking about pick your knitting needles up off the floor, you nasty whore, before you trip over them and hit your head on the coffee table.

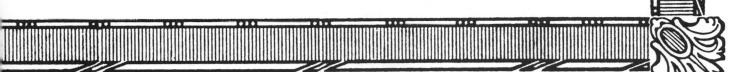

CUTS

a.k.a. You've Sliced the End of Your Finger off with a Rotary Cutter and Now You Are Bleeding All over Your Sister's Wedding Dress

Do:

1. Hold pressure. The idea is to stop the bleeding, not cut off the circulation. If you can, hold the injury above the level of your heart.

2. Clean gently with soap and water. If rebleeding occurs, try not to freak out. Hold pressure again.

3. Go to the emergency room if you cannot get the bleeding to stop.

4. If you develop signs of infection (pus, redness, etc.) go see someone.

Don't:

1. Panic. This should be self-explanatory, as it is difficult to take care of a spurting wound if you are passed out.

2. Attempt to cauterize the wound with a wood burner, not that I have ever heard of anybody being that stupid.

3. Try to use SuperGlue to reapproximate the edges. It stings like hell and if you do it at home it could get infected.

PUNCTURE WOUNDS

a.k.a. "Where Is My Needle? Oh, Never Mind, It Is in My Foot."

Do:

1. Make sure the entire item is out of your body.

2. Make sure your tetanus vaccine is up to date, unless you really enjoy having every muscle in your body contract at the same time.

3. Clean area with soap and water.

4. Go see your healthcare provider if you develop signs of infection.

Don't:

1. Place obstructive barriers such as antibiotic ointment or aloe vera over puncture wounds. These can actually trap bacteria inside the wound, which might make your finger or foot rot off.

2. Squeeze, pick, or otherwise taunt the wound. Again, this is an infection risk.

BURNS

a.k.a. You Had to Get a Woodburner for Christmas

Do:

1. First, allow cool water to run over the burn, especially if glue or other hot liquid is on your skin. It is not a bad idea to keep a vessel of cool water nearby when working with craft tools that use heat.

2. Cleanse with soap and water as gently as possible.

3. Cover with a loose bandage, even if a blister develops.

4. Go see your healthcare provider if the burn is over a joint, larger than 1" (2.5cm) in diameter, or begins to turn red and nasty.

Don't:

1. Put butter, petroleum jelly, or aloe on wound, as it can increase the risk of infection. Antibiotic ointment is OK as long as it is fresh from the drugstore and has not expired.

2. Pick the blister off. It can be uncomfortable to keep on but it is way better than gangrene.

3. Drink and glue. Alcohol is not our friend while wielding a glue gun or other craft tool. Use the lowest temperature setting possible.

Now these are just guidelines, not the gospel. If something looks funny and you are worried about it, you should see someone who is qualified to take a look, and by this we don't mean your next-door neighbor who happens to be a vet tech. It is always better to be overcautious than to let something go and wind up loosing a limb. Though I suppose you could always use your mad craft skills to make yourself a prosthetic limb . . . .

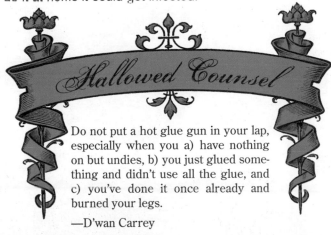

Hallowed Counsel

Do not put a hot glue gun in your lap, especially when you a) have nothing on but undies, b) you just glued something and didn't use all the glue, and c) you've done it once already and burned your legs.

—D'wan Carrey

TREE OF LIFE AND DEATH

BY ANDREA L. STERN

Celebrate life, or remind yourself of its brevity, with this fully beaded shrine. A wooden base provides the support for over-the-top bead embroidery embellishment done separately on a fabric sandwich before being attached to create the completed piece. Use your favorite fancy beads, found objects, or family mementos. Just what is hiding in that canopy of fruit-filled leaves? Could that be a lizard coming to tempt you?

MOOD ENHANCERS:

Thick as a Brick by Jethro Tull

SKILLS USED:

Basic beading

Beaded backstitch (see project instructions)

MATERIALS AND TOOLS:

Wood triptych, preferably round top, 7" × 9" (18cm × 23cm) when opened, or wood and screws to make triptych of this size (see pattern)

Rubber lizard

Rubber giraffe

2 animal beads

Bird bead

Bone skull bead

100 8mm x 6mm leaf beads, with hole across top

50 assorted fruit beads (apples, oranges, pears, grapes)

1 white disc bead, preferably shell

50–60 4–6mm assorted light blue rondelle style beads

12 5mm light blue round beads

1 package assorted blue 6/0 beads

1 package assorted blue 11/0 beads

1 hank transparent dark aqua 11/0 beads

1 hank light green opaque 11/0 beads

1 hank dark green opaque 11/0 beads

1 hank dark green iridescent 11/0 beads

4 hanks assorted brown 11/0 beads (4 shades of brown)

1 hank #2 bugle beads in brown

1 package/hank size 13/0 or 15/0 seed beads

NOTES:

Peltex does not shrink up when beading the way a lighter-weight interfacing will. If you cannot find the Peltex, or prefer to use a different interfacing, allow for some shrinkage of your finished piece and leave a larger seam allowance when preparing the base. It is also possible to bead directly onto the Peltex without applying the fabric first—I just like the effect of using a colored fabric beneath the beads.

2 packages 4mm Lochrosen Swarovski crystals, in crystal AB

1 package 6mm flat blue sequins

¼ yard (23cm) Peltex or 40 weight Pollon interfacing

¼ yard (23cm) cotton fabric in a blue to coordinate with your sky colors

Golden's Acrylic Tar Gel Medium

Beading needles, size 12

Thread, Silamide, C-Lon, or Nymo, in color to coordinate (I used Light Gray Silamide)

Pencil

Scissors

Beeswax

Sewing machine

For back (optional)

Jacquard Lumiere paint in Halo Blue/Green

Photo of Earth as seen from space, or other planet

3 rubber fish

1 bag of shell chip beads

1 jar BeaDazzles rubber stamping embellishment beads in turquoise

1 small florist's pic of flowers or fruit of your choice

1. Using the triptych as a template, trace a center piece and two doors onto the Peltex with a pencil.

2. Iron your fabric and fold, right sides together. Pin the Peltex to the fabric. Sew along your traced lines, using a short stitch length. Trim the fabric and Peltex close to the seam. Make a slit in the center of the fabric, and turn the piece right side out. If you desire, sew again around the edges to stabilize the piece while you sew on beads.

3. Following the template, draw the tree and landscape onto the fabric. Make sure the doors are placed properly.

4. Starting with the tree, place the lizard in the center. Attach him by sewing over the legs. Outline his silhouette with beads, using backstitch. Come up through the fabric, string four to six beads, go into the fabric, then come back up two to three beads in and sew through those beads again. It may be helpful to draw stitching lines to follow if you desire a contoured look in your tree. Fill in the tree shape by sewing consecutive lines of brown beads until the shape is filled. Vary the colors for more interest and to give a more realistic look to the bark. Sew an apple and a skull bead at the base of the tree.

5. Switch to the green iridescent beads and outline the tree canopy. Some of these beads will have to go over the tree limbs you've already beaded. That's fine, it will give the tree canopy a more full look, just use more beads in your backstitch to reach over the limbs. Follow the dotted lines on the tree pattern and fill in the area by sewing consecutive lines of the green beads.

6. Using the light green and green beads, fill in the landscape by sewing the beads in a patchwork pattern. Depending on the size of the beads, the squares may be four beads high by four rows of beads wide. Vary the squares for more interest, with an eye to the proportions of light beads to dark beads. Sewing the squares in different directions gives a bit more texture to the grass. Sew an animal to the right of the tree.

7. Sew in the sky. Start by sewing a 5mm round bead wherever you'd like. Sew a rondelle on both sides of the round bead, using the sequin stitch. Sew a 6/0 bead, then a Lochrosen crystal. Sew a row of the 11/0 beads around that, then make consecutive rows of the beads to fill in the space. Use the bigger beads where you desire to add more texture and movement to the sky. Curved lines can be used to represent clouds. Use as many or as few of the bigger beads as you like.

8. Bead the two side panels in the same way, starting with the tree area and moving toward the sky. For these you will not need to bead a tree canopy, just sew a few of the leaf beads at each end of the branches, adding a bird and some fruit on the branch of your choice.

9. To fill in the tree canopy, bring your needle up through the end of the first row of green beads at the bottom of the canopy. Sew through three beads, thread three beads and a leaf, then three beads, then sew through three beads. Follow this pattern across the row, choosing a fruit bead instead of a leaf bead at random intervals. When you get to the end of the row, sew back through the fabric sandwich and then come up two rows above and sew back the other way, adding beads all the way across in the same manner. The beads will flop around at first, and waxing your thread will help prevent tangles. The results are definitely worth it.

10. For the base, sew branch fringe from the ends of the lines of beads that make up the tree. Come up through the fabric sandwich and through the last three to four beads on the tree. String fifty-one beads and sew back through the first four to five beads on the row, leaving a stop bead at the end that you do not sew through. String six beads and sew back through five, into the row of fifty, continuing this way until you reach the top of the fringe. Sew through a few beads and back into the fabric.

11. Attach the pieces to the shrine base by using a heavy-duty adhesive or Golden Acrylic Tar Gel Medium. Press together and let dry completely.

12. If desired, paint the back with the Jacquard Lumiere. Using a palette knife or other spreading device, make a layer of tar gel at the base of the shrine and fill in with the shell chip beads. Pour the BeaDazzles over that and pour the excess off. Let dry and then join your collage items using the Golden Tar Gel. When dry, set your shrine up on a firm level surface and enjoy!

Designer bio:

To read about Andrea, see page 114.

7" H
Center Panel
cut 1 out of wood
cut 1 out of Peltex
Side Panels
cut 2 out of wood
cut 2 out of Peltex
4.5" W
2.25" W

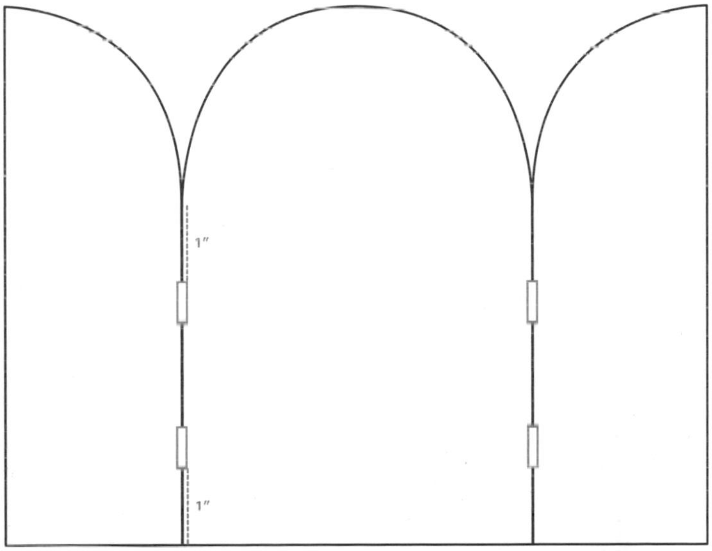

1"
1"

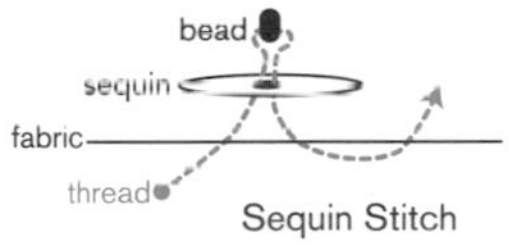

bead
sequin
fabric
thread

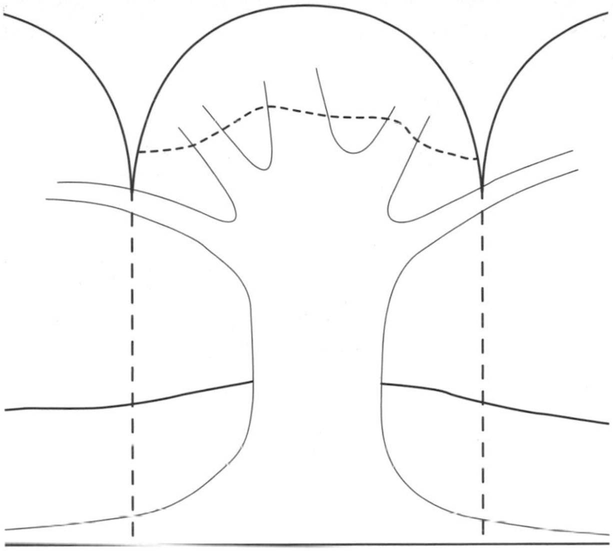

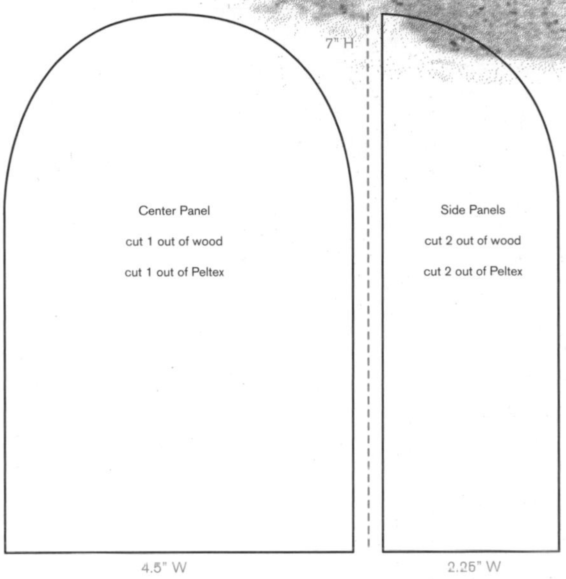

Sequin Stitch

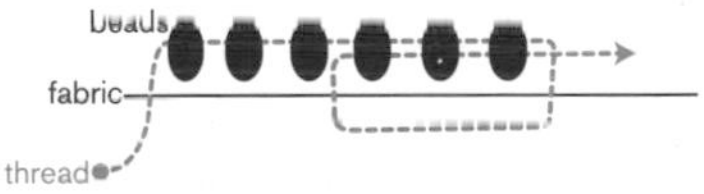

beads
fabric
thread

Backstitch

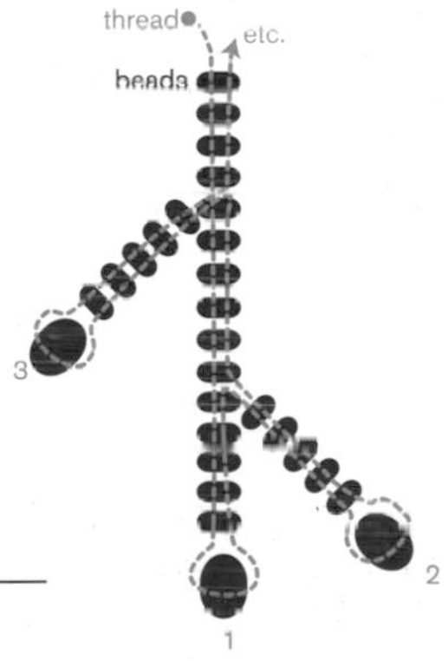

thread
etc.
beads
3
2
1

Branch Fringe

Hallowed Counsel

Jewel-It or The Ultimate are great glues for attaching found objects to your project.

—Andrea Stern

GRAFFITI

BY JACINTA LODGE

You know how there are always these cheap but horrifically ugly needlepoint tapestries hanging about, usually with pictures of fruit bowls or galloping stallions? Well why not use these as the perfect canvas for a bit of graffiti?

MOOD ENHANCERS:

Basquiat (1996; rated R)

SKILLS USED:

Basic cross stitch

MATERIALS AND TOOLS:

Painted/printed tapestry canvas
6-stranded cotton embroidery threads in:
Bright Red (DMC 666)
Bright White (DMC 5200)
Sea Mist Blue (DMC 747)
Waterfall Blue (DMC 3811)
Grapefruit Yellow (DMC 744)
Tangerine Orange (DMC 741)
Electric Blue (DMC 3844)
Cloud Blue (DMC 3756)
Lagoon Turquoise (DMC 598)
Pale Yellow (DMC 3078)
Light Tangerine (DMO 742)
Orange (DMC 740)
Needle
Scissors
A needle threader if you're uncoordinated

Getting started:

Find the center of the canvas by measuring, counting, or folding, and mark it by sewing a little bit of thread through. By starting from the middle (marked by arrows on the pattern's sides) you won't run out of space on one side accidentally.

Preparing the thread:

Stranded cotton, like DMC or Anchor, comes with six threads. For most tapestry grids you need a thickness of four threads. Cut about 20" (51cm) from the six-stranded threads and then pull the individual threads apart by pinching the top and pulling one through your fingers. Put back together however many you need. Doing it like this stops them from getting all knotty and twisted when stitching.

Sneaky ways of starting stitches:

It's all well and good to say just start stitching—but really, how do you do that? Here's a couple of ways to head off on that very first stitch.

The Waste Knot: Knot the end, go through from the front a few inches (or centimeters) from your first stitch, and then start cross-stitching. As you go, cover this tail with stitches and then snip the knot off! Done!

The Loop Start: useful for even numbers of threads. It's a bit more tricky, but an absolute snap once you get the hang of it. When you first prepare the thread, cut it twice as long as you need. Then take two individual threads, double them over and thread the all ends through the needle together. Now you have four strands with a loop at the bottom. Start from the back and bring the needle forward through the fabric, leaving some dangling out the back. Then finish that half-stitch by going back through the fabric. Slip the needle through the loop and pull tight—and Voilà!

Just start stitching:

So, um, just start stitching. Follow the chart and outline your finished work with a nice backstitch. Remember to only use four strands of floss at a time. See *Finishing Off* (page 128) for what to do when your needle runs out of thread.

Backstitch

Okay, so the rules kinda say that you are meant to do proper backstitch when outlining cross-stitch. This is a stitch where you always come up through the fabric at the far end of each stitch and then bring it back down where the stitch started. You then bring the needle up at the end of the next stitch and so forth. So you work your way forward going backward. Sound reasonable? Not to me either! So you know what? I cheat and just do a running stitch most of the time! Really, just sew the outline any way you like—it just has to leave a line on the front after all. The only thing to remember is to use just one strand of floss.

Finishing off:

To finish a thread, simply pass it under the back of the stitches you've already made. Still worried it may come undone? Then, going in the other direction, go under the backs of the next line of stitches and it won't budge.

Designer bio:

Jacinta Lodge is a displaced Australian living in Berlin, Germany, and after seven years is still not entirely sure why. Despite masquerading as a mild-mannered research scientist during daylight hours, genetic manipulation and hazardous chemicals just didn't bring all the thrill she needed. Therefore, to increase the overall knife-edge quality of her life, she's started a cross-stitch design business called Stitchalicious (www.stitchalicious.com). These designs are partly her own work and partly that of other young artists creating a weird mix of iconic street art and cool cartooning, styles never before rendered into cross stitch and just what the crafting community is screaming for. Because, let's face it, if there's one thing embroidery needs it's some serious funking up.

Jacinta spends most of her spare time trying to excel at pub trivia quizzes, teach her German husband the art of irony and train her mongrel dog to balance cookies on his head. She's currently failing dramatically at all three, but not yet ready to give up.

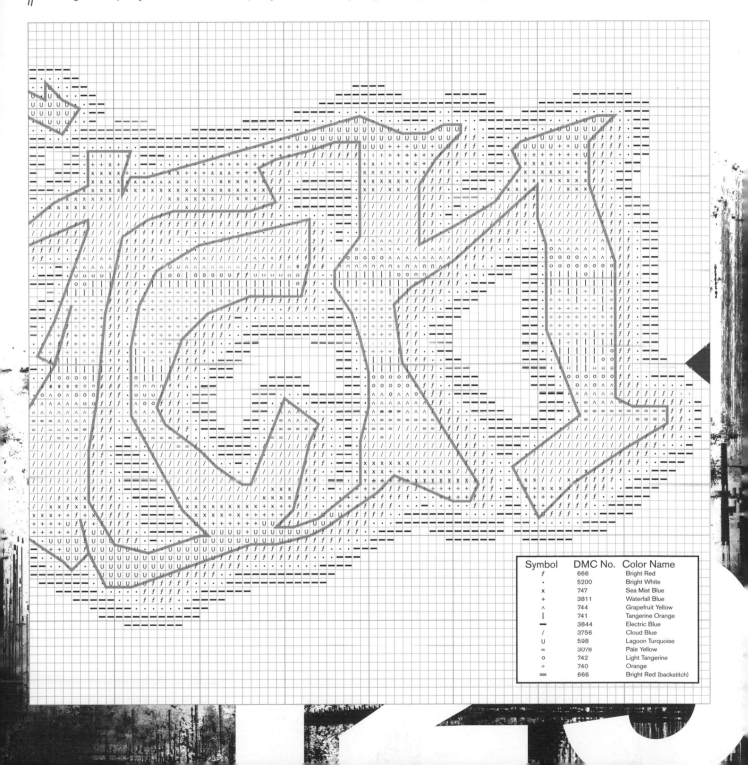

Symbol	DMC No.	Color Name
ƒ	666	Bright Red
.	5200	Bright White
x	747	Sea Mist Blue
+	3811	Waterfall Blue
^	744	Grapefruit Yellow
I	741	Tangerine Orange
▬	3844	Electric Blue
/	3756	Cloud Blue
U	598	Lagoon Turquoise
=	3078	Pale Yellow
o	742	Light Tangerine
+	740	Orange
▬	666	Bright Red (backstitch)

Techniques for Virgins

Master List of Abbreviations

Knitting

BO bind off

CC contrast color

Dec decrease

Inc increase

K knit

K2tog knit two together

Kfb knit into front and back

M1 make one

MC main color

P purl

P2tog purl two together

Pm place marker

Psso pass slipped stitch over

Pu pick up

Rnd round

RS right side (outside; side of the work that will show)

Sl slip (always slip purlwise unless told otherwise in the pattern)

Sm slip marker

Sp space

Ssk slip, slip, knit

Ssp slip, slip, purl

St stitch

W&t wrap and turn

WS wrong side (inside; side of the work that will be hidden)

Yo yarn over

Crochet

Adj adjustable

Bpd back post double crochet (imagine it as back treble post crochet for English)

Blo back loop only

Ch chain

Dc double crochet (same as English treble crochet)

Dec decrease

Ea each

Fpd front post double crochet (imagine it as front treble post crochet for English)

Flo front loop only

Hdc half double crochet (same as English half treble crochet)

Inc increase

Rem remain, remaining

Rep repeat

Sc single crochet (same as English double crochet)

Sk skip

Slst (or Sl st) slip stitch

Sp space

St stitch

Tc tapestry crochet

Tr treble crochet (same as English double treble crochet)

Yo yarn over

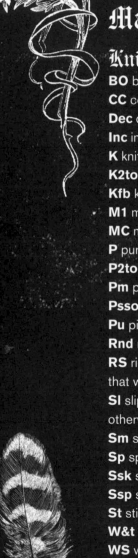

We here at *The AntiCraft* believe in brevity of instruction and complexity of design. To that end, we present only a rough course in how to do a majority of techniques in this book. If this section cannot teach you what you need to know, never fear, there is always the Internet. The Internet is your friend, except when it's stealing your identity and purchasing a small island off the coast of Illinois. Who knew your credit was that good?

Knitting

Slip Knot and Casting On

There are numerous ways of casting on, but for all of the projects in this book, the long-tail method will work just fine.

  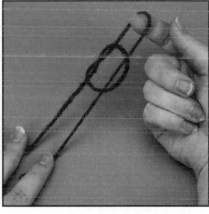

1. To make a slip knot, first make a pretzel with the yarn.

2. Hook the back strand with your index finger and lift up.

3. Hold the loose ends with your free hand and pull the hooked strand until the knot is snug.

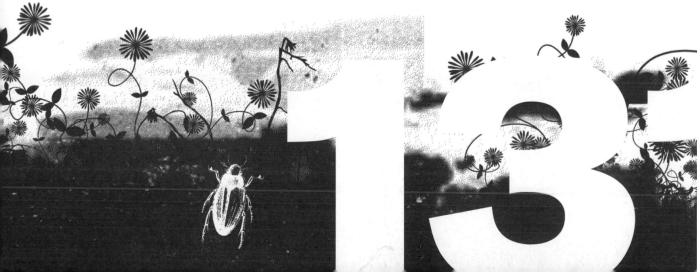

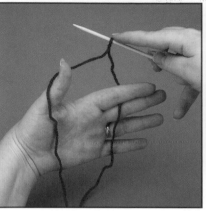
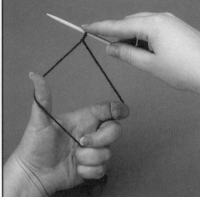

4. After making a slip knot with a long tail of yarn, insert one needle through the knot. Hold the knitting needle with slip knot between your thumb and index finger. Arrange the yarn so the long tail drapes behind the thumb and over the palm of your free hand, and the yarn leading to the skein goes behind your index finger and over remaining fingers.

5. Grasp both ends of yarn with the three remaining fingers.

6. Hold the slip knot in place on the needle with the right index finger. Slide the needle up the thumb (but under the yarn).

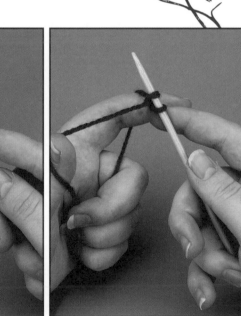

7. Continue holding the slip knot on the needle. Slide the needle down the index finger (but under the yarn), hooking a loop on the needle.

8. Pull the loop between the two strands of yarn held by the thumb. Release the yarn from the thumb.

9. Pull snug. Repeat from step 5 until you have cast on the number of stitches required. Eventually a rhythm appears and you can use your thumb to pull snug *and* set up the next cast-on stitch.

Knit Stitch (K)

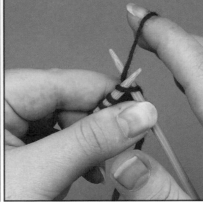

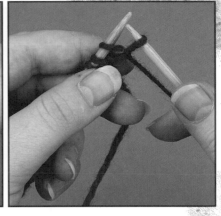

1. To make a knit stitch, hold the needle with the live stitches in your left hand and the empty needle in your right. Hold the working yarn behind the needles. Insert the right needle through the stitch on the left needle, as shown.

2. Wrap the working yarn counter-clockwise around the right needle.

3. Pull the wrapped yarn on the right needle forward and through the stitch on the left needle.

Purl Stitch (P)

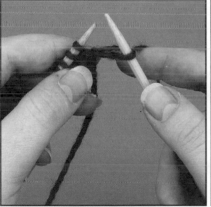

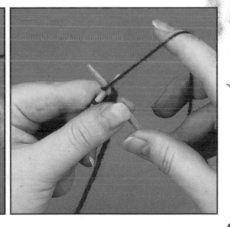

4. Drop the stitch from the left needle.

1. To make a purl stitch, hold the needle with the live stitches in your left hand and the empty needle in your right. Hold the working yarn in front of the needles. Insert the right needle from right to left through the front of the stitch on the left needle as shown.

2. Wrap the working yarn counter-clockwise around the right needle.

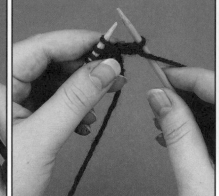

3. Pull the wrapped yarn on the right needle back and through the stitch on the left needle.

4. Drop the stitch from the left needle.

Garter Stitch

Knit every row to achieve this fabric.

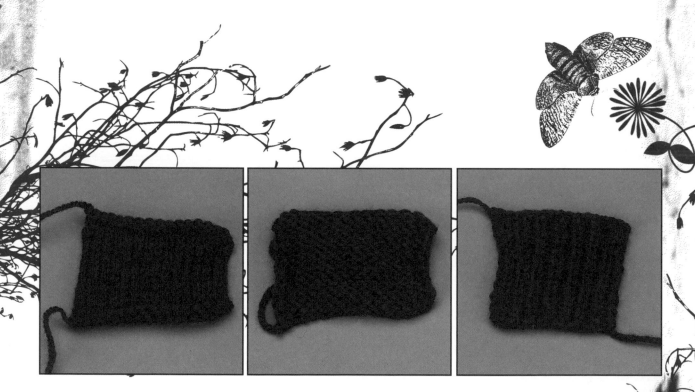

Stockinette Stitch

To achieve this fabric, alternate knit and purl rows. Notice how stockinette stitch naturally curls.

Reverse Stockinette Stitch

In truth, this is just the other side of stockinette. Yup, we flipped that swatch right over.

1 × 1 Ribbing

To create this fabric, alternate knit and purl stitches on the first row. On subsequent rows, knit the knit stitches and purl the purl stitches as they appear. For beginners, it's often easier to use a number of stitches divisible by two, which allows you to start with a knit stitch on every row.

Knit Two Together (K2tog)

1. Insert the right needle through the next two stitches on the left needle, as if to knit.

2. Wrap the yarn counterclockwise, as if to knit.

3. Pull the wrapped yarn on the right needle back and through the stitch on the left needle, as if to knit. (Get the feeling you're just knitting, but with two stitches together?)

Purl Two Together (P2tog)

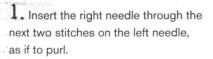 Insert the right needle through the next two stitches on the left needle, as if to purl.

2. Wrap the yarn counterclockwise, as if to purl.

3. Pull the wrapped yarn on the right needle back and through the stitch on the left needle, as if to purl. (Get the feeling you're just purling, but with two stitches together?)

Slip, Slip, Knit (Ssk)

1. Insert the right needle into the stitch on the left needle, as if to knit, but instead of knitting, just slip the stitch onto the right needle.

2. Slip another stitch as if to knit.

3. Slide the two slipped stitches back to the left needle. Notice they are now facing the opposite direction from every other stitch on the needle.

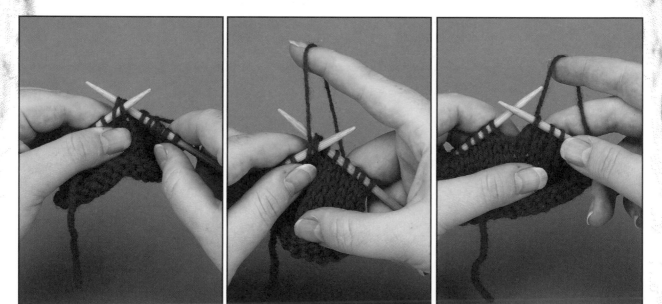

4. Knit through the back loop (kbl) of the two slipped stitches by inserting the right needle from right to left through the back of the stitches on the left needle.

5. Wrap the yarn counterclockwise, as if to knit.

6. Pull the wrapped yarn on the right needle forward and through the stitches on the left needle. Drop the stitches off the left needle.

Slip, Slip, Purl (Ssp)

 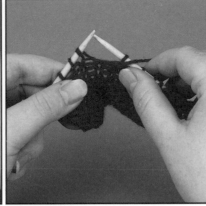 

1. Slip two stitches as if to knit (just as you did for ssk).

2. Transfer the slipped stitches back to the left needle.

3. Insert the right needle from left to right into the back of the slipped stitches. This may take some minor acrobatics.

Binding Off (BO)

Just as there are many ways to cast on, so are there ways to bind off. The method shown here is a simple way.

4. Wrap the yarn counterclockwise, as if to purl. Pull the wrapped yarn on the right needle back and through the stitches on the left needle. Drop the stitches off the left needle.

1. Knit the first two stitches.

2. Use the left needle to lift the first stitch up and over the second stitch.

3. Continue lifting the stitch off the right needle.

4. You now have only one stitch on the right needle. Knit another stitch and repeat steps 2–3 until only one stitch is left. Cut the yarn, leaving a long tail, draw the tail through the final stitch and pull it snug.

1. Pull the left and right needles slightly apart to see the horizontal bar connecting the two stitches on both sides.

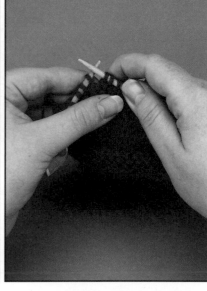

2. Using the left needle, lift the bar.

3. Insert the right needle from right to left through the back of the picked-up bar as if to kbl (see step 4 of Ssk) and wrap the yarn counterclockwise.

4. Pull the wrapped yarn on the right needle forward and through the picked-up bar on the left needle.

Knit into Front and Back (Kfb)

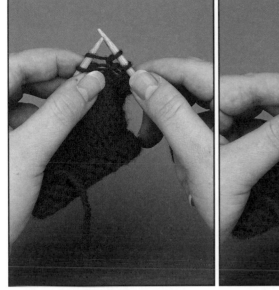

1. Knit a stitch as normal but do not remove the stitch from the left needle.

2. Kbl (as in step 4 of ssk) through the same stitch you just knit.

3. Drop the stitch from the left needle. Notice the increased stitch on the right needle. There will be a slight bump on the RS of the work with kfb.

Pick Up Stitches, Top (Pu, Top)

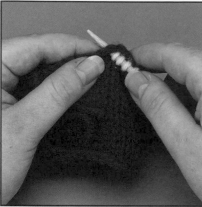

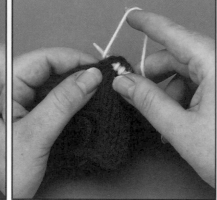

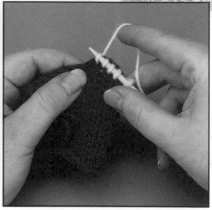

1. Insert the needle through the next stitch in the row below the bound-off edge. (Shown in contrasting yarn.)

2. Wrap the yarn counterclockwise, as if to knit.

3. Pull the wrapped yarn on the right needle forward and through the stitch on the left needle.

Pick Up Stitches, Side (Pu, Side)

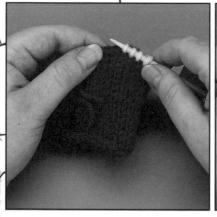

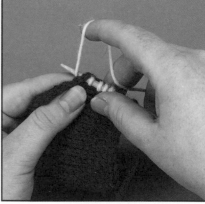

Stitches picked up along a bound-off edge. (Shown in contrasting yarn.)

1. Insert the needle through the stitch as shown. (Shown in contrasting yarn.)

2. Wrap the yarn counterclockwise, as if to knit.

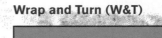

Wrap and Turn (W&T)

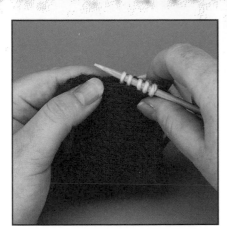

3. Pull the wrapped yarn on the right needle back and through the stitch on the left needle.

1. Knit until the point you are instructed to w&t. Slip one stitch from the left needle to the right needle as if to purl.

2. Next, move the yarn forward between the stitches.

3. Move the slipped stitch back to the left needle and return the yarn to the back.

4. Turn the work and complete the row as instructed in the pattern.

5. To pick up a wrapped stitch, knit to the wrapped stitch, pick up the wrap with the right needle as shown.

6. Knit the previously wrapped stitch and the picked up wrap together as one stitch.

1. To seam using mattress stitch, joining top to bottom, thread the yarn needle with yarn that matches your work. (Contrasting yarn is used here for visability.) With the pieces you are seaming laying RS up, insert the needle into the first two bars on one piece.

Double Knitting (DK)

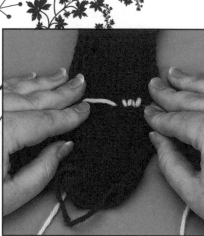   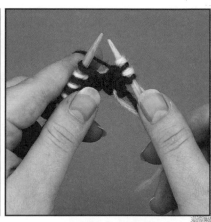

2. Next, insert the yarn into the first two bars on the second piece. Continue in this manner, alternating between the two pieces and pulling taut as you go. The stitches will disappear.

3. To seam using mattress stitch, joining side to side, follow instructions as for joining top to bottom, but instead work through the vertical knit stitches.

While double knitting, you can hold both working yarns in the same hand you normally use, or you can hold each yarn in different hands. The important thing to remember is when you are knitting the RS color, hold both working yarns to the back . . .

Double-Pointed Needles (DPN)

. . . and when you are purling the WS color, hold both yarns in the front. Otherwise, your double knitting will be inside-out (the smooth knit sides will be hidden on the inside and the bumpy reverse stockinette will show on the outside).

1. Cast on the desired number of stitches to one needle, then divide them evenly across the desired number of needles (three shown here) by slipping stitches from needle to needle.

2. Arrange the stitches so they are not twisted—that is, the bottom ridge of the cast on does not twirl around your needles, but instead lines up neatly.

Knitting in the Round

To join stitches in the round, take the needle that has the working and tail ends of yarn in your right hand. Hold the working yarn in your usual manner. In your left hand, take the needle that has the end of your cast-on stitches. With your right hand, pick up a fourth needle. Begin to knit the stitches from the left-hand needle onto the fourth needle. When you run out of stitches, transfer the empty needle to your right hand and begin again.

Intarsia

When knitting with the Intarsia method, you are working with multiple strands of yarn, usually wound on separate bobbins. No yarns are stranded across the back as with Fair Isle knitting.

1. To switch yarns using the Intarsia method, knit with MC until you are instructed to change colors.

2. Cross the CC yarn under the first strand of MC yarn.

3. Proceed to knit with the CC yarn.

4. Cross the second strand of MC yarn under the CC yarn when you reach the end of the CC section. Proceed to knit with the MC yarn.

1. Thread a yarn needle with the desired color yarn. Bring the point of the needle from WS to RS in the center of a V made by a knit stitch. Leave a tail long enough to weave in on the WS.

2. Pass the needle behind the two bars that make up the V of a knit stitch in the row above where you originally inserted your needle.

3. Insert the needle back into the starting point, RS to WS.

4. Pull snug, but not too tight or the work will pucker. Repeat as necessary from step 1 when you bring the needle from WS to RS to create your motif.

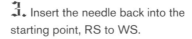

Chain (Ch)

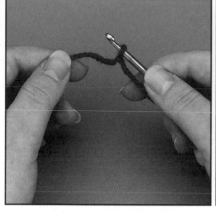
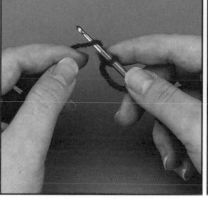

1. Start by making a slip knot (see page 131). Insert the crochet hook through the loop.

2. Holding the slip knot in place with your right hand, wrap the working yarn around and over the hook as shown.

3. Pull the wrapped yarn through the loop. Continue by repeating from inserting the crochet hook in step 1.

Single Crochet (Sc)

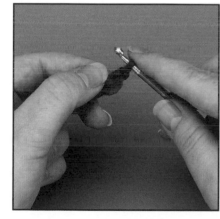
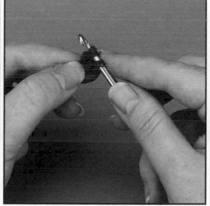
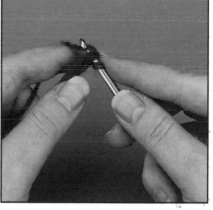

1. Chain a foundation row of the desired length.

2. Insert the hook through the two top loops in the second chain from the hook.

3. Wrap the working yarn around and over the hook as shown.

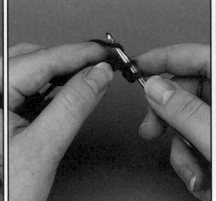

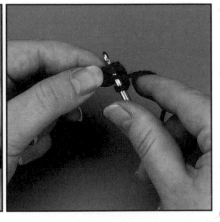

4. Pull the wrapped yarn through. You now have two loops on your hook.

5. Wrap the working yarn around and over the hook as shown.

6. Pull the wrapped yarn through both loops on the hook. You now have one loop on the hook. Continue by repeating from step 2 in the next chain stitch (*not* the second chain stitch from the hook).

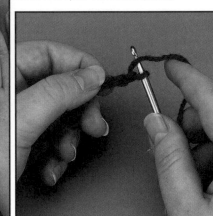

Half Double Crochet (Hdc)

Completed row of single crochet.

1. Chain a foundation row of the desired length.

2. Wrap the yarn around and over the hook, then insert the hook through the two top loops in the third chain from the hook.

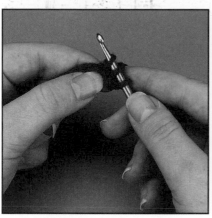

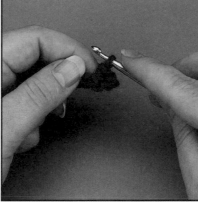

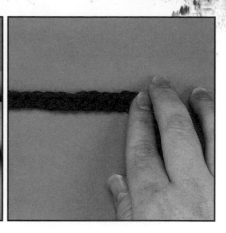

3. Wrap the yarn around and over the hook again and pull a loop through the stitch. You will now have three loops on the hook.

4. Wrap the yarn around and over the hook again and pull through all three loops on the hook. Continue by repeating from step 2 in the next chain stitch.

Completed row of half double crochet. Notice it is slightly taller than single crochet.

Double Crochet (Dc)

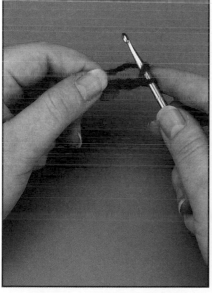

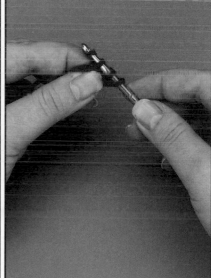

1. Chain a foundation row of the desired length. Wrap the yarn around and over the hook.

2. Insert the hook through the two top loops in the fourth chain from the hook. Wrap the yarn around and over the hook.

3. Pull the wrapped yarn through the loop. Wrap the yarn around and over the hook.

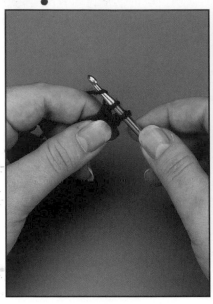 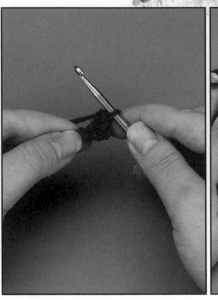 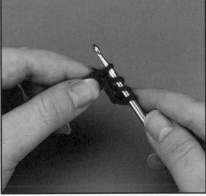

4. Pull the wrapped yarn through two loops on the hook. Wrap the yarn around and over the hook.

5. Pull the wrapped yarn through the remaining two loops on the hook. Continue by repeating from wrapping yarn in step 1 and crocheting into the next chain stitch.

Completed row of double crochet. Notice that it is slightly taller than half double crochet.

Treble Crochet (Tr)

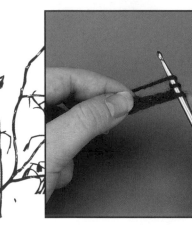 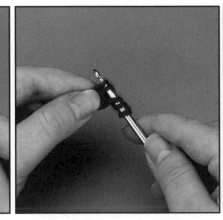 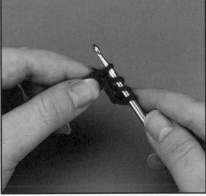

1. Chain a foundation row of the desired length. Wrap the yarn twice around and over the hook.

2. Insert the hook through the two top loops in the fifth chain from the hook.

3. Wrap the yarn around and over the hook and pull the wrapped yarn through the stitch.

Slip Stitch (Sl st)

Slip stitch is practically invisible when done in coordinating yarn. It is shown with contrasting yarn for clarity.

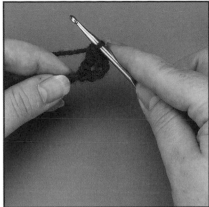

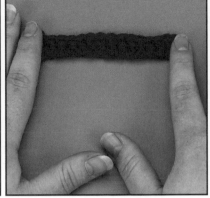

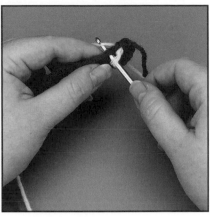

4. *Wrap the yarn around and over the hook and pull the wrapped yarn through two loops. Repeat from * until you have pulled through the last two loops and only one loop remains on your hook. Continue by repeating from wrapping yarn in step 1 and crocheting into the next chain stitch.

Completed row of treble crochet. Notice that it is slightly taller than double crochet.

1. You will already have one loop on the hook. Insert the hook through the next stitch. Wrap the yarn around and over the hook.

Single Crochet (SC) Decrease (Dec)

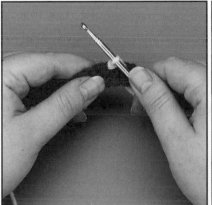

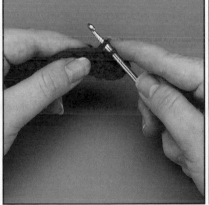

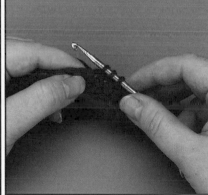

2. Pull the wrapped yarn through the stitch and loop. Continue by repeating from step 1.

1. Crochet to the point where you want to do a decrease. Insert the hook through the next stitch, wrap the yarn around and over the hook, and pull the wrapped yarn through the stitch.

2. Insert the hook through the next stitch, wrap the yarn around and over the needle, and pull the wrapped yarn through the stitch.

Double Crochet(DC) Decrease (Dec)

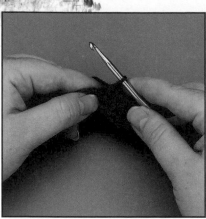

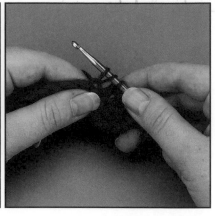

3. Wrap the yarn around and over the hook and pull through all three loops on the hook. You have one loop now on your hook and have decreased by one stitch.

1. Crochet to the point where you want to do a decrease. Wrap the yarn around and over the hook.

2. Insert the hook through the next stitch, wrap the yarn around and over the hook, and pull the wrapped yarn through the stitch.

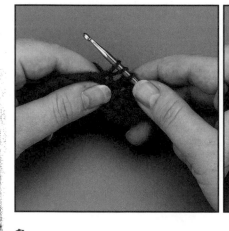

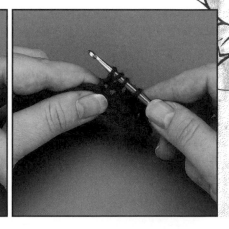

3. Wrap the yarn around and over the hook and pull the wrapped yarn through the first two loops on the hook.

4. Wrap the yarn around and over the hook.

5. Insert the hook through the next stitch, wrap the yarn around and over the needle, and pull the wrapped yarn through the stitch.

Front Post Double Crochet (Fpd)

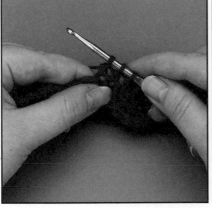

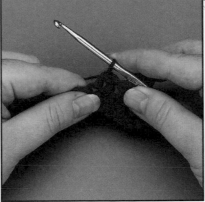

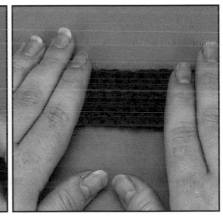

6. Wrap the yarn around and over the hook and pull the wrapped yarn through the first two loops on the hook.

7. Wrap the yarn around and over the hook and pull the wrapped yarn through the remaining three loops on the hook. You now have one loop on your hook and have decreased by one stitch.

1. Crochet to the point where you wish to begin fpd. Insert the hook around the vertical post directly below the next stitch as shown. Continue as if double crocheting until the stitch is complete.

Back Post Double Crochet (Bpd)

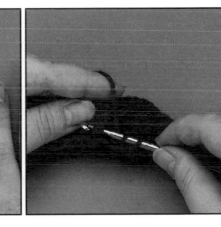

2. Notice that a fpd stitch is slightly raised compared to the surrounding dc stitches.

1. Crochet to the point where you wish to begin bpd. Insert the hook around the vertical post directly below the next stitch at the back of the work as shown. Continue as if double crocheting until the stitch is complete.

2. Notice that a bpd stitch is slightly recessed compared to the surrounding dc stitches.

Tapestry Crochet (Tc)

Tapestry crochet is worked in the same manner as single crochet, but you will be working with more than one color. The unused color is carried along the top ridge of the stitches.

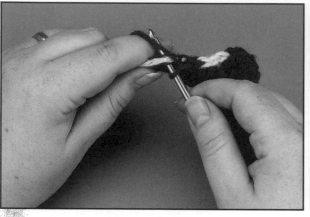 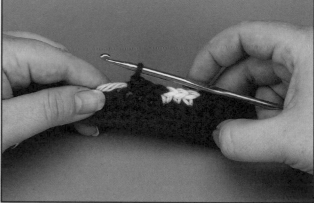

1. With the working yarn, make a single crochet over the carried color as shown.

2. When worked correctly, the carried yarn should not be visible between the stitches.

Changing Color in Tapestry Crochet

1. With the first color, begin a single crochet by inserting the hook through the stitch, wrapping the yarn around and over the hook, and pulling the wrapped yarn through the stitch. With the second color, wrap the yarn around and over the hook.

2. Complete the single crochet using the second color.

3. You are now working with the second color yarn. Continue working in single crochet, carrying the first color yarn along the top ridge of the stitches.

Circular Flat Peyote Stitch

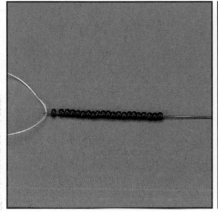
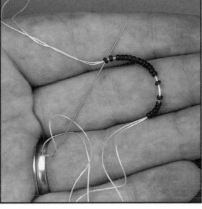

1. Thread a beading needle with appropriate thread. String the starting number of beads onto the beading thread.

2. Connect the beads into a circle by threading the needle into the first bead you strung in the previous step.

3. Pull the thread taut to form a ring.

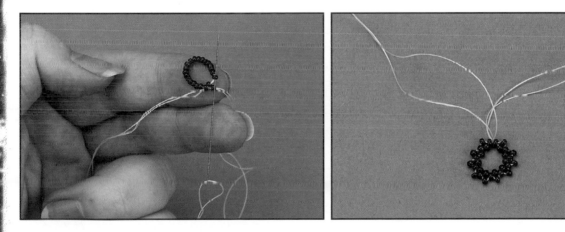

4. Thread a new bead onto the needle. Skip the next bead in the closed ring and insert the needle into the following bead.

5. Pull taut. Continue adding new beads as described in step 4 until you have completed the round. You will end up with a ring that has alternating beads and spaces like the one shown here.

Starting with Jump Rings

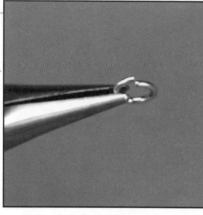
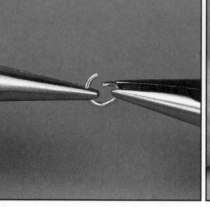
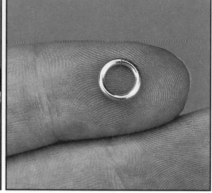

This is a chainmail jump ring. As packaged, they are neither fully opened nor closed.

To work with jump rings, you need two pairs of needle-nose pliers. Do not use pliers with teeth, as they will mar the ring. To open a jump ring: Hold one pair of pliers in each hand, and use the pliers to grasp both sides of the ring, leaving the opening in the middle. Twist the sides of the ring in opposite directions to open it. Never pull a ring open—you want your hands to stay the same distance from each other as when they are holding the ring. A ring pulled open will never properly close.

To close a jump ring: Hold one pair of pliers in each hand, just as you did to open the ring, and grasp each side of the ring, leaving the opening in the middle. Twist the sides of the ring in opposite directions inward and push the sides together slightly to close it. You will want the opening of the ring to disappear as much as possible—the sides should fit snugly together. Notice in this photo how the seam of the opening is barely seen. If the jump ring is properly closed, you will not be able to feel the seam when you run your finger over it.

European 4–1

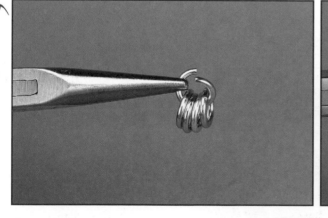
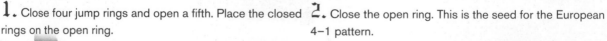

1. Close four jump rings and open a fifth. Place the closed rings on the open ring.

2. Close the open ring. This is the seed for the European 4–1 pattern.

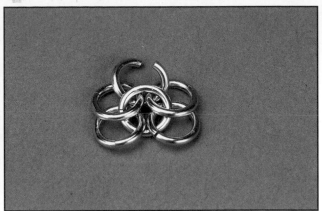

3. Lay the chainmail on a flat surface and arrange the rings until they lay as shown. The top part of the middle ring will be laying on top and appear to be pointing away from you. The side rings will lay with their bottoms pointing toward you.

4. Add an open ring through the topmost right- and left-side rings. Do not thread it through the middle ring. Arrange the ring so that it will lay they same way the middle ring lays when it is closed.

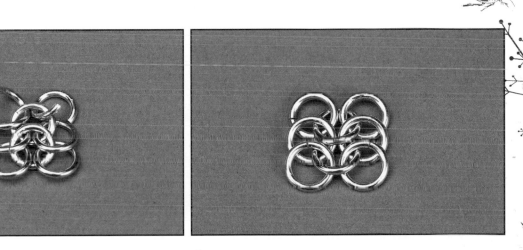

5. Close the middle ring. Next, add an open ring to both the left and right sides. (You are adding two rings total.) You will want to thread the open rings through the ring you just closed (now the topmost middle ring) and through the topmost ring on the side you are on. Arrange the rings so they will lay the same way the side rings lay when they are closed.

6. Close the ring you just added. Check your work to make sure all middle rings appear to be pointing toward you and all side rings appear to be pointing away, as in this photo. Repeat from step 4 until you have the length you desire—this is called a ribbon chain. There are many ways to connect seeds or expand them into sheets of chainmail (some are more time- and motion-efficient than others), and an Internet search for "European 4–1" will find them for you.

Educate Thyself

Knitting

- www.tinyurl.com/yo5ruf
  Elizabethan Stocking formula
- www.knittinghelp.com
  videos for right- and left-handed knitting techniques
- *The Art of Fair Isle Knitting* by Ann Feitelson
- *The Good Housekeeping Needlecraft Encyclopedia*
  edited by Alice Carroll
  (out of print but often available used)
- *The Knitter's Handbook*, from XRX Inc.
  color knitting/double strand knitting
- *Knitting School: A Complete Course* from RCS Libri
- *Stitch 'N Bitch: The Knitter's Handbook* by Debbie Stoller
- *Vogue Knitting Quick Reference Guide* from Sixth
  & Spring Books
  double points/knitting in the round

Crochet

- www.crochetme.com/assembling-amigurumi
- www.crochetme.com/content-type/tutorial
- www.crochetville.org
- www.futuregirl.com/craft_blog/2006/10/tutorial
  -seamless-single-crochet.html
- www.anniesattic.com
- www.tamemymind.com/artscrafts/pages/
  patternbooks-crochet-toysanimals.php
- *300 Crochet Stitches* (The Harmony Guides, V. 6)
  from Collins & Brown
- *220 More Crochet Stitches* (The Harmony Guides, V. 7)
  from Collins & Brown
- *Stitch 'N Bitch Crochet: The Happy Hooker*
  by Debbie Stoller

Tapestry Crochet

- www.tapestrycrochet.com
- http://iweb.tntech.edu/cventura/rightstitches.html
  tutorials with illustrations
- *Tapestry Crochet* by Carol Norton (Ventura)
- *More Tapestry Crochet* by Carol Ventura
- *Bead & Felted Tapestry Crochet* by Carol Ventura

Beading

- www.beadandbutton.com
  (search for "peyote stitch" or "beaded backstitch")
- www.robinatkins.com

Chainmail

- www.mailleartisans.org (the basics)
- http://cgmaille.com/tutorials.html (advanced)

Sewing

- www.futuregirl.com/craft_blog/2007/01/tutorial-hand
  -sew-felt.html
- www.lovetosew.com
- *Sewing 101: A Beginner's Guide to Sewing* from
  Creative Publishing International

Embroidery and Cross Stitch

- *The Embroidery Stitch Bible* by Bettie Barnden
- www.embroderersguild.com/stitch/stitches/index.html
- www.subversivecrossstitch.com/howto/index.html

Index

Acknowledgments

ZABET SAYS:

"I'd like to thank the Academy . . ." Get comfortable, 'cause I intend to go on and on and there's no producer to cut me off by going to commercial.

There are so many people who have had a hand in this book that I don't know if I'll be able to call them all by name. I'm also not sure where any of those hands have been before getting them in here. This book could be a festering germ playground, a bacterial utopia. Lick it at your own risk. (Pappas, I'll do it for a dollar and a White Russian.)

I want to thank my husband, Patrick, for being my anchor. He did a lot of behind-the-scenes help, everything from getting me a cup of tea to talking me down when I was freaking out.

I'd like to thank my family for their support. My parents are divorced and I know they are looking right now to see which one of them gets mentioned first, so therefore I am going to mention my brother first. Thank you, David, for saying "wow" and "good for you" at all the right times when I called to tell you we had gotten this book deal, even though I know you were thinking, "Punk-goth craft book? My nerdy little sister? She's kidding, right?" As for my dear parental units, you have contributed to this venture equally, but in entirely different ways. I love you both and I know you love me, no matter what other areas in our lives where our opinions might differ.

I'd like to thank all the friends I neglected while trying to get this thing together. I appreciate your patience. Also, to everyone who let me vent at them about the process, I owe you. Big time. The following people may be a member of either the former or the latter group, and the truly unfortunate managed to get in both: Brittany, Bug, Carrie, Colleen, Erik, Gigi, Heather, Jane, Janis, Josh, Kaye, Kim, Mary Beth, Pappas (the Lame Pirate), Raellyn, Robyn, Sarabeth, Sarah, Shannon, Tardy, and Terry. Hummus on me!

Last, but in no way least, I want to thank Renée for being my partner in crime, though I know at some point we probably just wanted to strangle each other. This book thing has been like learning to ride an ostrich, and we've survived. Go us!

RENÉE SAYS:

My fellow graduates from Delicate Flower Finishing School know, deep in their hearts, that the most important thing is to never thank anyone for anything. Thanking someone admits that you are beholden to them for your success. And no Delicate Flower ever depended on anyone. If I were, though, to humble myself and give thanks, first it would have to be to the designers, who were willing to put their devious creativity on these pages. Then, of course, I would have to thank the husband of doom and greatness, Matt, for offering valuable insight as to when we were actually being funny, and when we just had our heads shoved in dark places. Then, of course, the unicorns. I would thank the unicorns. And Zabet for putting up with me. And rainbows. And my family. And our strange and discontent world for giving me something to focus my energies upon. And Sug Sams. But most of all, I would have to thank all our readers. Thank you, each and every one.

WE'D BE REMISS IF WE DIDN'T SAY:

We have more people to mention. The girls at the genesis of this AntiCraft stuff: Lori, Sarabeth, Sharon; Deb Stoller for her encouragement; the folks at North Light who made a book happen: Tonia, Maya, Greg, Tim, Al, and everyone who touched this book; the amazing designers who loved their projects enough make them beautiful and were brave enough to let them go; Pat and the staff at 3rd Street Café, where we made liberal use of free WiFi and thought we were at our funniest; Kim, for her lawyer's eye; the ReBelle girls, Robyn and Sarah, who let us have The AntiCraft's birthday party at the store; Raellyn for her last-minute help; Brenda and Christine, who talked us up in their podcasts (caston.com and pointysticks.org, respectively); and the Google Overlords. Every single one of you did something that made this book better.

We are astounded and appreciative.

Renée is a rehabilitated failing writer in Lexington, Kentucky. She is kept company by a husband, who seems to dig her particular brand of crazy, and a son, who is rapidly following in her footsteps. She knits, crochets, cooks, and writes, saves her pennies for home improvement projects, and is way cooler than this bio makes her sound.

Zabet is a polyglot, Hispano-Celt, design geek, general freak, and feminist who took out her tongue stud in 2003. She lives with four cats (crazy), one husband (geeky), and a library filled with binders of her poetry (bad). She also knits too much, saves her pennies for a tubal ligation, and isn't nearly as cool as this bio makes her sound.

Together, they form a dynamic duo dedicated to eradicating the forces of happiness and light from the modern crafting world via their website TheAntiCraft.com.

FEED YOUR CREATIVE URGES WITH THESE OTHER DELECTABLE NORTH LIGHT TITLES

DOMIKNITRIX

Jennifer Stafford

Whip your knitting into shape. Inside *DomiKNITRix*, you'll find a no-nonsense, comprehensive guide to essential knitting operations and finishing techniques, including step-by-step instructions for all the basic stitches used in the book. Then get your hands dirty with over 20 spicy projects to satisfy any knitting appetite. Projects range from smaller items like naughty candy heart pillows and a mohawk hat to larger, more complicated pieces like the L'il Red Riding Hoodie and a men's sweater vest with an anatomically correct skull. Just let the *DomiKNITrix* show you how it's done.

ISBN-10: 1-58180-853-4
ISBN-13: 978-1-58180-853-7
flexibind • 256 pages • Z0171

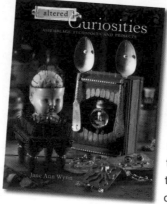

ALTERED CURIOSITIES

Jane Ann Wynn

Discover a curious world of assemblage and jewelry with projects that have a story to tell! As author Jane Ann Wynn shares her unique approach to mixed-media art, you'll learn to alter, age, and transform odd objects into novel new works of your own creation. Step-by-step instructions guide you in making delightfully different projects that include jewelry, hair accessories, a keepsake box, a bird feeder, and more—all accompanied by a story about the inspiration behind the project. Let *Altered Curiosities* inspire you to create a new world that's all your own.

ISBN-10: 1-58180-972-7
ISBN-13: 978-1-58180-972-5
paperback • 128 pages • Z0758

KALEIDOSCOPE

Suzanne Simanaitis

Get up and do something creative! *Kaleidoscope* delivers your creative muse directly to your workspace. Featuring interactive and energizing creativity prompts ranging from inspiring stories to personality tests, doodle exercises, purses in duct tape, and a cut-and-fold shrine, this is one-stop-shopping for getting your creative juices flowing. The book showcases eye candy artwork and projects with instruction from some of the hottest collage, mixed-media, and altered artists on the Zine scene today.

ISBN-10: 1-58180-879-8
ISBN-13: 978-1-58180-879-7
paperback • 144 pages • Z0346

ALTERNATION

Shannon Okey and Alexandra Underhill

Hey you, indie-crafter... yeah you, crafty chick with the scissors. Check out *AlterNation*, the DIY fashion Bible, that shows you how to personalize your wardrobe with a wide range of no-sew and low-sew techniques. This book has lots of cool stuff to make, like a tie skirt, T-shirt dress, scrap scarf, and oh so much more. Just follow the step-by-step instructions, and you'll soon be a total pro at making your own clothing and accessories.

ISBN-10: 1-58180-978-6
ISBN-13: 978-1-58180-978-7
paperback • 144 pages • Z0713

THESE TITLES AND OTHER FINE NORTH LIGHT BOOKS ARE AVAILABLE AT YOUR LOCAL CRAFT RETAILER, BOOKSTORE OR FROM ONLINE SUPPLIERS.